D1373331

Extraordinary Jobs in

MEDIA

ALECIA T. DEVANTIER & CAROL A. TURKINGTON

Ferguson
An imprint of Infobase Publishing

Athens Regional Library
2025 Baxter Street
Athens, GA 30606

Extraordinary Jobs in Media

Copyright © 2007 by Alecia T. Devantier and Carol A. Turkington

All rights reserved. No part of this book may be reproduced or utilized in any form or by any means, electronic or mechanical, including photocopying, recording, or by any information storage or retrieval systems, without permission in writing from the publisher. For information contact:

Ferguson
An imprint of Infobase Publishing
132 West 31st Street
New York NY 10001

Library of Congress Cataloging-in-Publication Data

Devantier, Alecia T.
  Extraordinary jobs in media / Alecia T. Devantier and Carol A. Turkington.
    p. cm. — (Extraordinary jobs)
  Includes index.
  ISBN 0-8160-5860-1 (hc : alk. paper)
  1. Mass media—Vocational guidance. I. Turkington, Carol. II. Title. III. Series.
  P60.D48 2006
  302.23023—dc22   2006011389

Ferguson books are available at special discounts when purchased in bulk quantities for businesses, associations, institutions, or sales promotions. Please call our Special Sales Department in New York at (212) 967-8800 or (800) 322-8755.

You can find Ferguson on the World Wide Web at http://www.fergpubco.com

Text design by Mary Susan Ryan-Flynn
Cover design by Salvatore Luongo

Printed in the United States of America

VB KT 10 9 8 7 6 5 4 3 2 1

This book is printed on acid-free paper.

CONTENTS

ACKNOWLEDGMENTS

This book wouldn't have been possible without the help of countless others who referred us to individuals to interview and came up with information about a wide variety of odd and unusual jobs. We deeply appreciate the time and generosity of all those media experts who took the time to talk to us about their unusual jobs.

Thanks also to all the people who helped with interviews and information, including Susan Shelly McGovern and Jon Rand.

Thanks also to our editors James Chambers and Sarah Fogarty, to Vanessa Nittoli, to our agents Ed Claflin of Ed Claflin Literary Associates and Gene Brissie of James Peter Associates.

ARE YOU CUT OUT FOR A CAREER IN MEDIA?

Some kids spend hours surfing the Internet, perfecting their Xanga site, or communicating via Facebook or instant messages. Other kids love playing piano, dance, modern music, or ceramics. But then there are some kids who just seem to be born with a pen in their hand and a nose for news—these are the kids who excel in English and writing class. If this sounds like you, you're probably the only one in your English class who doesn't moan when your teacher assigns an essay. You already may be working for your school paper or yearbook, or maybe you've signed up for journalism or creative writing. If you're really lucky, your school also offers a radio or TV production studio where you can get hands-on practice.

Are you fascinated with uncovering what's really going on in your hometown? What's the city council really up to? What scandals are local businesses trying to sweep under the carpet? Can you imagine a better way to spend an afternoon than fooling around with the latest desktop publishing software, or figuring out how to alter the images on your new digital camera?

If you're passionate about words, current events, writing, and communication, a career in the media may be just what you're looking for. Of course, there's a lot more to a career in the media than sitting behind a desk and reading the news. You may be interested in being a newscaster or a journalist, but don't forget there are tons of other job possibilities in the media beyond a news desk or a newspaper reporting slot. If you like to write but you're also a born critic, you might consider a career crafting film, restaurant, or movie reviews. Maybe you love the business of communication, but you'd rather manage people than write the news. You'll find lots of opportunity in administration as an editor or producer in TV, radio, and print.

If you're a little more offbeat than buttoned up, you might consider a career writing humor, political satire, or astrology columns. There are all kinds of production possibilities as well—including cameraperson, lighting expert, layout artist, and more.

Take some time to think about the kind of person you are, and the sorts of experiences you dream of having. Are you passionate about politics, news, the environment, or women's issues? Do you love to write or take photos? Do you have a hunger to be the first with the newest information? Do you love being on the inside? Are you passionate about the fundamental right of a free people to know the truth, no matter what the cost? A career in the media might be just perfect for you.

Of course, if you're thinking about this type of career, you'd better be a hard worker, because many of these jobs require incredible dedication and very long hours. Working in this field may seem glamorous and exciting—and it often is—but that thrill comes at a price. When everyone else is out partying or relaxing, you'll be the one working holidays, nights, and weekends. You've got to be ready to follow the story wherever it takes you, for as long as it takes. That can make it hard to combine a career in media with a home and a family.

Getting that first job is another challenge. Some kids figure they'll graduate after four years in college and find the world's TV and newspapers just waiting on their doorstep. But unless you're related to Bob Woodward or Katie Couric, it may not be that easy. Breaks are hard to come by, and most people in the media start out on the bottom, in out-of-the-way places on tiny TV or radio stations or weekly newspapers. It can take years to break into the big-city newspapers, magazines, and national stations or networks.

Breaking into the field is only one problem. Some kids have inherited a lot of *shoulds* in thinking about the kind of person they want to be. These *shoulds* inside your head can be a major stumbling block in finding and enjoying a job in the media. You'll also need to realize that there may be other people who aren't so happy with your career choice. You may hear com-

plaints from your family and friends who just can't understand why you don't want a job with more "regular" hours and better pay. This is especially true for those in the TV business, where the success rate for landing a job can be depressingly low. Many never make it to that national news chair. If you confide your career dreams to some people, you may find they try to discourage you. Can you handle their continuous skepticism?

Think about these things carefully, but don't cheat yourself. Remember, if you're born with a dream, you owe it to yourself to go after it, no matter how unusual, odd, weird, or just plain batty it may seem to others. If you don't do what you were born to do—well, you're going to get older anyway. You might as well get older doing what you love to do. Working in the media isn't necessarily an easy career, but if you allow yourself to explore the options that are out there, you'll find that work and play often become the same thing. Push past your doubts and fears, and let your journey begin!

Carol A. Turkington
Alecia T. Devantier

HOW TO USE THIS BOOK

Students face a lot of pressure to decide what they want to be when they grow up. For some students, the decision is easy, but for others, it's a real struggle. If you're not interested in a traditional 9-to-5 job and you're eyeing the media as a unique way to make a living, where can you go to learn about these exciting, nontraditional jobs?

For example, where can you go to find out how to become a TV meteorologist? What does it take to become a world-traveling photographer for *National Geographic*? Where do you learn how to be a humor columnist? Is it really possible to make a living as an astrology columnist? Where would you go for training if you wanted to be an editorial writer or a cable TV sports personality? What's the job outlook for a TV reporter?

Look no further! This book will take you inside the world of a number of different jobs in the media, answering questions you might have, letting you know what to expect if you pursue that career, introducing you to someone making a living that way, and providing resources if you want to do further research.

THE JOB PROFILES

All job profiles in this book have been broken down into the following fact-filled sections: At a Glance, Overview, and Interview. Each offers a distinct perspective on the job, and, taken together, give you a full view of each job.

At a Glance

Each entry starts out with an At a Glance box, offering a snapshot of important basic information to give you a quick glimpse of that particular job, including salary, education, requirements, personal attributes, and outlook.

- *Salary range.* What can you expect to make? Salary ranges for the jobs in this book are as accurate as possible; many are based on the U.S. Bureau of Labor Statistics' *Occupational Outlook Handbook*. Information also comes from individuals, actual job ads, employers, and experts in that field. It's important to remember that salaries for any particular job vary depending on experience, geographic location, and level of education.
- *Education/Experience.* What kind of education or experience does the job require? This section will give you some information about the types of education or experience requirements the job might require.
- *Personal attributes.* Do you have what it takes to do this job? How do you think of yourself? How would someone else describe you? This section will give you an idea of some of the personality traits that might be useful to you if you choose this career. These attributes were collected from articles written about the job, as well as recommendations from employers and

people actually doing the jobs, working in the field.

✓ *Requirements.* Are you qualified? You might as well make sure you meet any health, medical, or screening requirements before going any further with your job pursuit.

✓ *Outlook.* What are your chances of finding a job in the media? This section is based in part on the *Occupational Outlook Handbook*, as well as on interviews with employers and experts. This information is typically a "best guess" based on the information that's available right now, including changes in the economy, situations in the United States and around the world, job trends, and retirement levels. These and many other factors can influence changes in the availability of jobs in the media.

Overview

This section will give you an idea of what to expect from the job. For most of these unusual careers, there really is no such thing as an average day. Each day is a whole new adventure, bringing with it a unique set of challenges and rewards. This section will give you an idea of what a person in this position might expect on a day-to-day basis.

The overview also gives you more details about how to get into the profession, offering a more detailed look at the required training or education, if needed, and providing an in-depth look at what to expect during that training or educational period.

No job is perfect, and **Pitfalls** takes a look at some of the obvious and maybe not-so-obvious downsides to the job.

Don't let the pitfalls discourage you from pursuing a career; they are just things to be aware of while making your decision.

For many people, loving their job so much that they look forward to going to work every day is enough of a perk. **Perks** looks at some of the other benefits of the job you may not have considered.

What can you do now to start working toward the career of your dreams? **Get a Jump on the Job** will give you some ideas and suggestions for things that you can do now, even before graduating, to start preparing for this job. Opportunities include training programs, internships, groups and organizations to join, as well as practical skills to learn.

Interview

Each entry features a discussion with someone who is lucky enough to do this job for a living. In addition to giving you an inside look at the job, this interview provides valuable tips for anyone interested in pursuing a career in the same field.

APPENDIXES

Appendix A (Associations, Organizations, and Web Sites) lists places to look for additional information about each specific job, including professional associations, societies, unions, government organizations, training programs, forums, official government links, and periodicals. Associations and other groups are a great source of information, and there's an association for just about every job you can imagine. Many groups and associations have a student membership level, which you can join by paying a small fee. There are many advantages to joining an association, including the chance to make important contacts, receive helpful newsletters, and attend workshops or conferences. Some associations also offer scholarships that will make it easier to further your education.

In **Appendix B (Online Career Resources)** we've gathered some of the best general Web sites about unusual jobs in the media, along with a host of very specific Web sites tailored to individual media jobs. Use these as a springboard to your own Internet research. Of course, all of this information is current as we've written this book, but Web site addresses do change. If you can't find what you're looking for at a given address, do a simple Internet search—the page may have been moved to a different location.

READ MORE ABOUT IT

In this back-of-the-book listing, we've gathered some helpful books that can give you more detailed information about each job we discuss in this book. Find these at the library or bookstore if you want to learn even more about jobs in the media.

ADVICE COLUMNIST

OVERVIEW

It may seem easy, sitting around in your pajamas thinking up snappy answers to readers' problems, but professionals who do this for a living take their job very seriously. After all, advice columnists get paid to do what just about everybody loves to do for free—and that's give advice and nose into other people's problems. Two of the world's most famous advice columnists—the late Ann Landers and her sister Abigail Van Buren (both pen names), blazed the trail of best-known advice givers whose tart yet sensible replies set the standard for advice columnists across the country. Ann Landers, who sometimes wrote her columns from her bathtub, called herself "the general manager of the world," which pretty much describes the types of questions an advice columnist might be called upon to answer.

Whether it's marital problems, young love, or which way to roll the toilet paper, advice columnists gather a whole host of questions from readers and try to come up with interesting replies. Most well-known advice columnists are syndicated, which means they work for a company that sells their column to newspapers around the globe.

Advice columnists may differ in the exact way they handle the job, but in general, each day the columnist surveys some of the most interesting letters (often sifted through first by assistants) and then chooses several letters to answer for one column. The columnist tries not to answer the same question over and over, but looks for questions that have universal appeal and that may strike a chord with many readers. But the day doesn't stop there. Many of the best-known advice columnists also write books and appear all over the country as guest speakers, entertaining and informing audiences.

AT A GLANCE

Salary Range
$30,000 to $1,000,000+

Education/Experience
Although most columnists are expected to have a degree in journalism, English, or communications, advice columnists don't absolutely have to have college degrees or traditional journalism backgrounds. Still, you're better off with a degree, preferably in journalism or another communications major.

Personal Attributes
You should have a genuine interest in helping others, boundless curiosity, excellent research skills, and be outgoing and comfortable interacting with all kinds of people. You'll need a thick skin to handle complaints from people who don't like your advice, or who think they could do better.

Requirements
You'll need a clear, lively, friendly, warm, and witty writing style, with a sure sense of the pulse of your reading public. You'll need to know the kinds of problems your readers have and know the sources who can give you information about obscure problems. You also need to be able to meet deadlines, and write quickly and with style and flair.

Outlook
Fair to poor. There are very few openings or opportunities for advice columnists. The most successful columnists are syndicated, but syndication is difficult to achieve.

Harlan Cohen, syndicated advice columnist

Harlan Cohen is one of the youngest (and the only male) syndicated advice columnists in the country, whose *Help Me, Harlan!* column is read by more than 4 million fans a week. A former reporter for his college paper at Indiana University, Cohen got the idea for an advice column while interning with *The Tonight Show with Jay Leno*. Back on campus after the internship, he founded an advice column, and he's been answering heartfelt letters asking for advice ever since.

Today, his column is syndicated by King Features and appears in local daily and college newspapers, including the *Dallas Morning News*, the *Seattle Times*, the *Pittsburgh Post Gazette*, the *St. Paul Pioneer Press*, and south Florida's *Sun-Sentinel*. He's also written for the *Wall Street Journal Classroom Edition*, the *Chicago Tribune*, and *Chicken Soup for The Teenage Soul III*, and he's been featured in the *New York Times*, *Psychology Today*, and *Seventeen*.

"I really wanted to be able to affect people, to have an impact," he says. "Initially, I wanted to reach people through humor, and the advice column was a vehicle to do that."

After he graduated from college, he noticed that local newspapers around the country were trying to attract younger readers, but there wasn't anything in the paper to engage their interest. "I put together a media kit, [and] made appointments with some newspaper editors within a two-hour driving radius." They all rejected him. "But I was able to figure out how to hone the column, to make it more desirable." Deciding to self-syndicate, he dropped 50 media kits in the mail and got five clients.

"It was ridiculous in a good way," he laughs. "I had 10 to 15 clients for about eight years." In the beginning, he says, it was never about making money. With six clients in those days before e-mail, it cost him $8.75 to send out hard copy and a disk to each client—but he was only getting paid $5 each for the column. "But it was creating a forum and establishing a voice, and I was doing it day in and day out," he says.

Unable to expand his client base, he called columnist Mike Royko for advice. "I couldn't get through to him," Cohen says, "so finally I called during lunch when I knew his assistant would be out. He picked up the phone." Boldly, Cohen asked the notoriously cranky Royko for column advice. "You just have to write," Royko snapped, "and write, and keep writing."

So that's what Cohen did.

"Luckily I always had enough clients," Cohen says. "Every time I got rejected by [an] editorial director, I wouldn't get angry. I'd call them up and ask them what could I do to improve." He ended up forming relationships with many of these editorial directors.

Then came his big break: Ann Landers died, and suddenly a thousand newspaper spots opened up. "I'd established enough of a voice and a following so I was offered a syndication deal, and the column continues to thrive, he says. "I'd still like it to grow. As big as it could possibly be, I know I'll continue to write and write.

"You have to do what you love to do. You have to get comfortable and confident with your voice and abilities. The only way you do that is by doing it, surrounding yourself with great people who will tell you the truth. They will be brutally honest with you, but [they] will be brutally on your side. You gotta believe in yourself, get great people around you to help support you."

One of the most challenging things about being an advice columnist is that so many people want answers. "The way the forum is designed, I can't answer everybody's question," Cohen explains. He's turned to writing books as a way of answering all those questions he can't get to in his columns, incorporating the different themes he has learned from the people who write to him. "There are a lot of books I want to write," he says. "The problem is they need an answer in two weeks, and the book is coming out in two years."

It's not always easy. "The actual writing part isn't delightful," he says. "It's a process, a means to get the information out there. I want to help people so that at least they know there is someone out there who cares. Each person is unique, but I try to keep the dialogue moving with different topics. I can't have every week be a dating and relationship issue. The unique questions are those that are deeply honest and are universal and are under 300 words. When those pop up, you're like: 'Yes!'"

Originally, his column was geared towards a younger audience, but today it engages people of all ages "Those readers who have wisdom, I love for them to share their stories and experiences," he says. "It's a forum that focuses on a lot of firsts—first love, first loss, first time battling with independence, dealing with sex, alcohol—but then you have all these people who have gone through it many, many times. What's great is, it's an adult conversation. You get parents who respond, kids who respond."

When one reader asked Harlan about the meaning of life, he responded that the short answer is that it's like a gas tank. "The more you live life, the more you can fill up that tank," he says. "Our only job is to continue to live life, to fill up that tank."

Cohen has also written *The Naked Roommate*. "It's really hit a nerve, it's become the number one book on college life." At the University of Texas, the book is required reading.

He spends a lot of time on college campuses, speaking to students and parents, and offering leadership workshops. "You need to find other ways to share information you're able to acquire," he says. He thinks the struggle to succeed was helpful. "It was the best gift ever," he says. "One thing I tell younger people—we really don't need to be in a hurry." Instead, he recommends taking the time to figure out what you want to do. "I don't need to be running myself ragged," he says. "I can discover something I love to do." He suggests you write for your school paper, since it's the easiest opportunity you'll have to get your words in print. "It's harder to get work once you graduate, to get those thoughts into print. A campus newspaper is just an amazing opportunity, and a lot of times they don't have enough people to write."

The key, he tells students, is to persevere. That's how he got the internship with Jay Leno—when he was told the studio wouldn't interview interns for several months, he kept calling every day until they gave in and granted him an interview. He got the internship.

"There are going to be a lot of people who tell you you're no good," he says. "Unless you've got people around you to tell you: 'You're not good, but you'll get better'—you won't get better.

"I like to tell kids to do what you love to do, be persistent, have great people around you, and know what you want to do and why you love doing it. I like being able to help people, and I love that someone can read [my column] and know they are not alone. Those moments you feel most alone, when in reality we are really part of the largest community in the world. Because we've all been there. To know that, and to see it, is to help someone in the most powerful way."

Most would agree that the hardest part about being a columnist is breaking in. Syndicating an advice column is extremely difficult, since there are a limited number of outlets for the column. Some columnists get around this by "self-syndicating"—which means you need to find your own clients and handle the distribution and billing yourself. The Internet has opened up more opportunities for potential advice columnists and bloggers, but the opportunity for making a living as an advice columnist is still best for those who get their writing into national newspapers.

Pitfalls

It can be tough landing a job in this field. The competition is keen and the opportunities fairly limited. Unless you can syndicate your column, you'll probably spend more on postage and disks than you'll earn. People who don't like what you've written about them may threaten to complain to your boss or cancel their newspaper subscription. You may have to argue with your editor to allow you to discuss a topic in your column that might be considered too controversial.

Perks

If you genuinely like to help people and you're a persistent, curious sort who loves to write, you can have a wonderful job reaching out to others and really feeling as if you're helping and educating the public. If you manage to syndicate your columns, you can do very well financially, especially with collateral work such as speaking fees, personal appearances, books, and newspaper articles.

Get a Jump on the Job

If you've got a yen for writing and you love to give advice, you can start as early as high school, writing an advice column for your school newspaper. Continue these efforts in your college paper, and take as many writing courses as you can. Think about getting an internship on a newspaper or with a syndication company.

AP WIRE SERVICE STAFFER

OVERVIEW

"Get it fast, get it first, get it right," is the motto of the Associated Press, the world's dominant news service. That motto is one of the few things that remains constant about the AP in an era of rapidly changing news technology. The AP was created in 1848 and became a central news agency that distributed stories to hundreds of newspapers. Today the AP has expanded its services to broadcasters and Internet providers. Until the early 1990s, the AP was the leader among three wire services that included United Press International and Reuters. UPI, another U.S.-based agency, serviced mainly afternoon newspapers and declined when those papers began disappearing. Reuters, based in London, still provides some general news but financial information has become its primary emphasis.

The AP is a news cooperative because newspapers and broadcasting outlets subsidize the wire service through paid memberships. If you have any doubt about the AP's importance and reach, just check how many stories in your local newspaper each day carry the AP byline. These stories are sent out by the AP, and are written by AP staff members or picked up from member newspapers. The AP delivers news around the world 24 hours a day; its services include a digital photo network, a continuously updated online news service,

AT A GLANCE

Salary Range
$25,000 to $60,000.

Education/Experience
You should have a college degree in journalism, broadcasting, or another communications major. You'll probably need a few years of reporting at a newspaper or radio or television station before getting hired at a wire service bureau.

Personal Attributes
You'll have to be able to handle intense deadline pressure because wire services are always on deadline. You'll also have to write quickly without sacrificing accuracy. You'll have to get accustomed to staying busy all the time.

Requirements
You'll need a clear writing style and must know how to organize a story. You'll have to be available to work nights and weekends.

Outlook
Most well-known wire services are changing directions or downsizing. The Associated Press (AP) remains the only major global service that emphasizes general news content. The AP is here to stay, though, and cost-conscious newspapers are more frequently using AP stories instead of hiring their own reporters to write them. So if you're looking for a wire service job, the AP's your best bet.

a TV news service, and one of the largest radio networks in the United States. This expansion as a news provider also means a greater variety of jobs in the more than 240 AP bureaus that serve more than 120 countries. Yet the traditional bureau journalist remains an AP fixture. Because of the fast writing and versatility required, this is one of the most demanding jobs in journalism.

The bureau journalist is expected to report and edit stories and sometimes cover a beat. While the AP's Washington bureau will keep more than 150 staffers to cover the federal government and national news, most bureaus maintain skeleton staffs. So if you're a newsman or newswoman in most bureaus, your routine will keep you hopping. Let's say you work from 8 a.m. to 5 p.m. (the "day desk trick"). Most bureaus are responsible for reporting all state and local news. Some bureaus, especially in state capitals, write their own stories. But the AP is entitled to pick up any stories from member newspapers, from which it obtains most of its content. So the first thing you'll do when you arrive at the bureau in the morning is check local newspapers and radio, and television and online news. You'll put together a news budget of all the stories that your bureau needs to provide for local AP members and

Scott Charton, AP staffer

Scott Charton was such a newshound that he landed a radio job at a 250-watt station in Morrilton, Arkansas, before he even had his driver's license. Charton couldn't have the job, however, unless he could drive to work, so he had to wait three weeks before turning 16 and getting his license. "I always wanted to be a news reporter," he recalls. "They were an AP broadcast member and I was fascinated. I wondered, 'Where's this news coming from?' In 1978, we had a tornado that killed some cows and I called the AP in Little Rock and they used the story. I was so thrilled. I knew then what I wanted to do and had to figure out how to do it." Because of health problems in his family, Charton left college to take a radio job in Louisiana. He then joined the AP bureau in Little Rock in 1983 as the broadcast editor, responsible for providing broadcast content to member stations. That was the start of a 22-year career in which Charton primarily covered state government for AP bureaus in the capital cities of Little Rock and Jefferson City, Missouri. Charton enjoyed state politics, including Governor Bill Clinton's administration in Arkansas, because the AP covers statehouses with its own reporters.

"The statehouse has always been the backbone of the AP," Charton says. "When visiting reporters would come to Jefferson City, the first place they'd want to stop would be the AP office. Big papers have people there year-round but the smaller papers do not. As long as there was statewide interest, at every board and commission meeting, for all the delegates in the House and Senate, our AP political reporter was there. I was in the press gallery one night for an 11 o'clock debate with the understanding that I was staying to the end," he says.

Charton covered the Missouri legislature for 12 sessions, and then in 2001 became the AP's roving Missouri correspondent. That assignment gave Charton the freedom within the state to cover just about anything and go just about anywhere.

"I got to write about fun things," he says. "I didn't get completely out of political coverage. What I did was write about how pending legislation affected real people. I enjoyed that and I enjoyed being in rural areas. I wrote about Governor [Bob] Holden's inaugural party in 2001 and about how much it cost, which led him to apologize. I wrote about the best places to eat

the AP national wire in New York. You may rewrite newspaper stories from top to bottom or hardly edit them at all. As the day goes on, you'll have to update stories with late-breaking developments. In all cases, the punctuation, use of capital letters, and other style must conform to the *AP Stylebook*.

Member newspapers in your area usually will send you important stories they assume the AP will want even before they're published. Your bureau also will decide how to use its own reporters each day. AP reporters cover such beats as business, sports, entertainment, and politics. If your bureau is in a state capital, an AP reporter will cover every significant legislative matter. If your bureau is in a major league sports city, an AP reporter will cover every home game for every team as well as daily developments. Your stories will be transmitted by computer software, a dramatic improvement from the days when every newspaper in America had a bank

along Interstate 70. And one of my last stories was about the move to legalize noodling, which is catching fish with your bare hands. I tried to find a balance of features and hard news. That balance is never perfect and it's fun to try and find that."

As much as Charton thrived on AP assignments, he quickly realized that the job's demands didn't suit everybody. He started out with two other new employees and was the only one who survived. "One guy could write polished copy but he couldn't write it on deadline," Charton recalls. "Another guy was a librarian and he didn't last three months because he couldn't crank it out quickly enough. It's a lot faster-paced than a newspaper. I had friends at newspapers and they'd say, 'I couldn't do your job. I have to arrange my notes, sit down and think.' There's nothing more thrilling than watching your copy rolling out of the bureau when a good editor's assembling it. You're seeing news put together before the [news outlets] are. That's a thrill for any reporter."

Before the era of laptops, AP reporters routinely dictated news stories by phone. They'd look at their notes and try to compose a well-organized and coherent story as they dictated to an editor at the bureau. "I was taught," Charton recalls, "always run to the phone, and until you get to the phone, think, 'What's my lead? What's the most important thing that just happened?' It's a wire service thing. You don't see dictations anymore. But with new technology and the demand for faster copy, I think that old wire service ethic is coming back."

Charton took an unpaid sabbatical from the AP in April 2005 to work on historical research projects. He helped the Missouri Press Association tape interviews with old editors to get their recollections of bygone newspaper days. While he was on sabbatical, Charton was asked by University of Missouri President Elson Floyd to become director of university communications. Charton was a bit surprised because he'd written some unfavorable stories about Floyd.

It may have seemed a bit odd that Charton was taking a university job. Although he attended three colleges in Arkansas, Charton never received a degree. "Education maybe ends but learning never does," he says. At the AP, Charton got all the education he needed.

of noisy wire service machines. Typewriter ribbons would clank away as wire stories appeared line by line and editors stood around reading important stories as they moved. Now an editor just opens a computer file to read and edit the latest AP stories. The way AP reporters and editors gather the news hasn't changed much over the years, but the way the AP provides the news—that's an entirely different story.

Pitfalls

You may spend years working nights before you're assigned to the day desk. You may feel anonymous because newspapers often don't use an AP reporter's byline. You may struggle to gain respect as a writer because of the AP's traditional reputation for straightforward, no-frills reporting. Some bureau staffers remain bound to their desks. The deadline pressure and workload isn't suitable for everyone.

Perks

It's very stimulating to feel that you're at the heart of the nation's news gathering process. You'll be exposed to a wide variety of tasks and beats. Many reporters get the chance to travel. The pay and most benefits are competitive with most newspapers.

Get a Jump on the Job

Look through your daily newspapers at the number of stories with bylines from the AP or other wire services. How does their style differ from stories by the paper's own reporters? For more information about wire service jobs, check out the careers section on http://www.ap.org.

AUTOMOTIVE WRITER

OVERVIEW

Americans have a long-running love affair with their automobiles. Many of us think a lot about our cars. In some cases, people identify themselves with the type of cars they drive. Many auto enthusiasts spend a lot of time watching car racing, thinking about cars, talking about cars, and reading about cars.

Because there are many people who like to read about cars, there are automotive writers who write about everything concerning automobiles and the automotive industry in newspapers, Web sites, and magazines.

While some automotive writers are journalists who have moved from another area into automotive writing, or who write about cars and trucks in addition to other journalistic duties, some auto writers get into the business from the automotive side of the industry. You'll find automotive writers who have worked as engineers for car manufacturers and then shifted to writing. Automotive writers also count race car drivers and former race car drivers among their ranks. Some automotive writers are technical writers who write to specific audiences about topics such as automotive electronics, engines, gearboxes, or air-conditioning.

If you don't see engineering or race car driving in your future, however, then you'll probably get into automotive writing from the journalism field. But you won't go from college straight to a job as an automotive writer. Most of these specialized writers

AT A GLANCE

Salary Range

Salaries for automotive writers vary greatly. Some automotive writers produce a weekly column for a newspaper, while others are employed full time by automotive magazines. The average salary ranges between $39,100 and $64,750.

Education/Experience

Experience also varies, but you'll probably need a bachelor's degree in journalism or communications. Some people enter the field from other areas, such as engineering or race car driving.

Personal Attributes

Automotive writers should be curious and must be able to write well enough to communicate technical information clearly and in an interesting way. You should be knowledgeable about the basic mechanics of automobiles.

Requirements

You'll need to have a driver's license and a clean driving record. Some publications may require writers to belong to a professional organization of automotive writers. A college degree is usually required.

Outlook

The demand for automotive writers is expected to increase at an average rate of between 10 and 20 percent through 2012. Additional opportunities may become available as more and more automotive Web sites are established.

have put in their time as general assignment reporters before eventually moving into automotive reporting.

While automotive writers may report on many different subjects, including general industry news, how gas prices are affecting the sales of different types of cars, and new auto technologies, most automotive writers thrive on driving different cars and reporting on their performances. These types of articles are intended to introduce readers to the many vehicles that are available, and help them to decide on the type and price of vehicle that would best suit their needs.

Auto manufactures set aside fleets of vehicles specifically for automotive writers to drive and report on. They also have special employees who deal exclusively with journalists to help them schedule cars for evaluation and provide information necessary for their stories. It's the job of knowledgeable automotive writers to drive various cars and light trucks—usually for several days—and then report on various aspects of the automobile, including performance, gas mileage in city and highway conditions, comfort, driving enjoyment, and so forth. When the automotive writer has spent adequate time driving the car or truck, the vehicle is returned to the

Nick Yost, automotive writer

Nick Yost wrote a weekly column about new cars and trucks for 21 years for the Reading *Eagle*, where he served as city editor. He's driven and reported about more than 1,000 vehicles. Now retired from the newspaper, Yost is a freelance automotive writer, working out of his home in northern New Jersey.

He writes for Web sites, the *Washington D.C. Times*, and various magazines, and he's active in the International Motor Press Association, a New York City–based organization of about 500 journalists and representatives of the automobile manufacturing industry.

Yost's interest in cars is lifelong, and, coupled with his writing ability, makes him well qualified as an automotive writer. "The best thing about being an automotive writer is the ability to learn about and actually experience the many cars and light trucks available," Yost says. "Another big plus is the opportunity to be around other people who share your passion. There are very few wealthy automotive journalists, but there are a lot of happy ones."

Yost bought his first car for $100 when he was in college, and spent a summer driving and working on it. At the end of the summer he sold it to a young neighbor for $40 and returned to college. He has owned and leased a long line of vehicles since then. "When you really like cars, like I do, they tend to become your hobby," he says. "People with a passion for cars start early in life to build up a foundation of knowledge through family, friends, and just hanging out with other car enthusiasts. They also love to tinker with cars and tend to buy a lot of them, starting with inexpensive, used ones that pique their interest, and then working up to more expensive ones as their finances improve."

Yost advises anyone interested in being an automotive writer to be patient. Drive a lot, learn all you can about cars, and be on the lookout for a paper or Web site looking for an auto writer. Once you've located one, you'll need to be able to demonstrate that you can handle the job.

"There's no single way to get into this profession, or even a logical progression," Yost says. "Generally speaking, however, automotive journalists are people who have already demonstrated skills in other journalistic or automotive-related endeavors."

manufacturer and the writer arranges to get another one to test.

Perhaps because it's a relatively small group whose members share a passion, automotive writers tend to get to know and bond with one another. Many of them attend auto shows and manufacturer introductions, join organizations, and attend meetings and conferences to share stories, advice, and information.

Pitfalls

Jobs for automotive writers are relatively few and far between. Although average job growth in this field is expected, and more jobs may become available through Web-based opportunities, the number of automotive writers is quite small. You'll usually need to gain experience in another area of journalism before you can begin writing about automobiles and related topics. If you're trying to break into automotive writing on a freelance basis, it's likely that you'll need to supplement your income.

Perks

If you love cars and driving, what could be better than getting paid to write about them? Automotive writers get invited to auto shows and manufacturer introductions, giving them the opportunity to travel around the country, and sometimes the world. They also get industry news first, enabling them to keep up with what's going on and be at the top of the information curve.

Get a Jump on the Job

Start by learning all you can about cars by reading auto magazines and other publications. Pay special attention to the different writing styles and the contents of different types of articles. When it's time for you to start driving, be diligent about learning the right way to do it. Once you're licensed and have some driving experience under your belt, figure out a way to drive as many different cars as possible (only with the permission of the owners, of course). Maybe your uncle would let you drive his Saab 9-3 convertible, or your best friend's mom would let you test out her Passat. Driving different cars will give you an idea of the differences in handling, comfort, and performance. While you're learning about cars and driving, you also should be practicing your writing. Volunteer to write a car column for your school paper. Even if you don't get to drive and write about a different car, you could write about automotive-related issues that affect your age group.

CABLE TV SPORTS PERSONALITY

OVERVIEW

The idea of round-the-clock sports programming seemed far-fetched when the Entertainment and Sports Programming Network began broadcasting on September 7, 1979. Any sport worth watching already was covered by the major networks. Besides, they offered sports for free. Most fans couldn't understand why they should pay a monthly fee, especially for ESPN's early events such as tractor pulls, Australian Rules Football, and United States Football League games. When ESPN crews showed up at major sports events in the network's early days, nobody else seemed sure what ESPN stood for or what it was doing. That second-class status didn't last long.

ESPN in 1987 received rights to telecast Sunday night NFL games, and the network was on its way to revolutionizing sports on television. ESPN had more time slots for sports and a bigger commitment to them than anybody else. The network could telecast an event such as the NFL draft, which kills two days and attracts too narrow an audience to interest major networks. ESPN eventually had too many shows for one network and started ESPN2, nicknamed "the Deuce." The network also launched Spanish-speaking programming and the ESPN Radio network. All this expansion gave the network the flexibility to start NFL draft coverage on ESPN and switch to ESPN2 after the early rounds. ESPN's amazing growth was highlighted

AT A GLANCE

Salary Range
$200,000 to $1,000,000+

Education/Experience
You'll need a college degree. A major in broadcast journalism is a big plus. You'll usually start as a sports reporter or sports anchor at a local station. If you're a well-known former athlete, you'll have the advantage of inside expertise and name recognition. Many cable personalities have come from newspapers, where they learned to report, made valuable contacts, and became experts in at least one sport.

Personal Attributes
You need a flair for entertaining because cable TV sports programs are often a mix of news and entertainment. Cable personalities often have nicknames, favorite expressions, or distinctive styles. You'll want to have a friendly and likeable appearance to viewers. If you're a reporter, you'll have to be aggressive and competitive.

Requirements
You need a strong, clear voice and a solid on-camera presence. Reporters need good news judgment and interviewing skills. You'll be asked to provide a videotape of your previous television work.

Outlook
Sports programming on cable TV keeps growing by leaps and bounds. Cable networks will continue to seek new shows and new talent. More jobs have been created by specialty networks, like those devoted to pro football, golf, or hunting and fishing. As long as America's appetite for sports coverage keeps increasing, so should the jobs in cable TV.

when it acquired rights to telecast Monday Night Football starting in 2006.

Rival cable networks joined ESPN in creating a huge new market for sports anchors, reporters, play-by-play announcers, producers, and anybody else involved in sports programs. Major league baseball teams began telecasting big chunks of their schedules on regional cable networks. Sports including pro football, golf, hunting and fishing, and horse racing now have their own networks. Cable now claims some of the most recognizable and highly paid sportscasters in America. Anchors on ESPN's daily *SportsCenter* shows are among the nation's most popular TV sports personalities.

Although cable has created many broadcasting jobs, they have become harder to get. Cable sports networks in their infancy were logical places to start out, but now they mainly hire established broadcasters. And the competition is fiercer than ever for journalism graduates and

Hank Goldberg, cable TV personality

Hank Goldberg was nicknamed "The Hammer" while he was host of a radio talk show in Miami. He took over from Larry King, America's best-known talk show host, when King moved on to join CNN in 1985. "I was called 'The Hammer' because of the abrasive way I handled bad callers," Goldberg recalls. "When I succeeded Larry King, he gave me one bit of advice: 'Don't suffer the fools—nobody wants to hear them!' Larry would always hang up on them. I'd insult them first."

Goldberg entered the talk show business with a long sportscasting resume, including 15 seasons as an analyst on Miami Dolphin radio broadcasts. But he was fired by his station in September 1992 because Goldberg refused to cancel an interview with novelist Elmore Leonard. The station manager wanted Goldberg to keep discussing Hurricane Andrew, despite the fact that it had been talked to death over the previous three weeks.

Fortunately for Goldberg, ESPN executive John Walsh noticed a short note in *Sports Illustrated*, which, tongue-in-cheek, described Goldberg as another victim of Hurricane Andrew. Walsh hired Goldberg to use his football expertise on ESPN Radio. Goldberg then auditioned for an NFL studio show on ESPN2 before it was launched in 1993. But the show was aimed at a young male audience and Goldberg, who was middle-aged, needed a gimmick to survive the cut. He huddled with one of the network's consultants. "I mentioned 'The Hammer' personality and they thought it was a great idea," Goldberg recalls. "So they gave me a mallet. I'd sit on the set and in addition to giving the NFL news and making a few picks, if there was something negative going on, I could use the mallet."

"They moved me over to the main network after a year and asked me what I would like to cover besides football. I say: 'horse racing,' and [executive] Steve Anderson says, 'Nobody's ever asked for horse racing.' That was a whole new niche for me."

Goldberg's NFL coverage expanded to reporting on games, handicapping games on a show with former NFL running back Merril Hoge, and writing columns for ESPN.com. Goldberg also has been host for a daily three-hour radio call-in show in Miami, which rounds out a very busy routine.

"On Monday, before my radio show, I watch *SportsCenter* in the morning," he says. "I'm on at 7, so when the show's over I try to make some calls, follow up on [local or national] news and broadcast professionals because so many ex-athletes join cable networks as game analysts and studio commentators. These jobs are so popular that ESPN in 2004 had 10,000 contestants for *Dream Job*, a reality series that offered the winner a one-year contract as an anchor on SportsCenter.

Cable sports networks also have expanded to radio and the Internet to broadcast games and deliver news. This opens multimedia opportunities for versatile journalists. A cable personality may report on a live event, offer analysis on radio, and write a story for the network's Web site. This routine, needless to say, can be exhausting and requires plenty of energy. As a testimony to cable television's willingness to cover just about any sport or game, the 2004 comedy film *Dodgeball* featured a fictitious broadcast crew from

occasionally break a story. I'm pretty well connected. Wednesday, I start working on my picks. I spend a lot of time on that. Thursday afternoon, they give me the order of games I'm going to pick with Merril on Friday night and ask me what video I want to go with each game. If I've got a game to cover, I leave early Saturday morning, fly into a city, go right to a team's facility and work with a producer to put together a piece for the Sunday morning [NFL] *Countdown* show."

Because he works for an all-sports network, Goldberg doesn't have to worry about talking over any viewer's head. "The people who are watching are sports fans and diehard ones at that," he says. "The proliferation of cable opportunities has created so much work, it's expanded the universe of sports broadcasting. It's a good thing, too, because local sports TV has become two sound bites and a score. That's all you get to do. You don't get to display what knowledge and personality you have on local TV any more."

Goldberg gets the chance to display both when he's trying to pick winners of NFL games and major horse races. He worked for Jimmy "The Greek" Snyder, who was once the best-known pro football handicapper in America. Goldberg enjoyed one six-week stretch on ESPN when he had a 25-4-1 record beating the point spread on NFL games. One Las Vegas sports book manager told Goldberg that customers would crowd around the TV on Sunday mornings to find out what Goldberg had to say. "They were betting my picks—that made me a little nervous," he says. "You feel like you're carrying the nation's economy on your shoulders. I think people who watch me get the sense that I'm one of them. I'm not some tout trying to make money. I'm the one guy who's accountable. Every weekend they post my record from the previous week. I've had gamblers ask me how I hold up under the pressure. The Greek used to say, 'If you're a player, you're born again every day.' "

Sometimes a stranger will get obnoxious with Goldberg because of a wrong pick. "But most people are nice and it's great when people recognize you," he says. "Some people give you a hard time for one reason or another. I never thought I'd be in a position like that." Goldberg never thought he'd be in the movies, either, until humorist Dave Barry asked him to appear in the 2005 comedy, *Complete Guide to Guys*. In the movie, based on a Barry novel, Goldberg plays himself giving the sports news.

Who ever knew "The Hammer" could have such a light touch?

ESPN8, nicknamed "the Ocho." That was supposed to be funny, but in truth, it may have revealed the wave of the future.

Pitfalls

Being easily recognized can have its downside. You may have trouble finding privacy at a restaurant or grocery store. While most people probably will be friendly, others can be obnoxious. If you report for a 24-hour cable sports network, you're liable to get a call any time of day or night when there's breaking news.

Perks

Your visibility will be more of a help than a hindrance. It will improve the cooperation you get from sports executives, coaches, managers, and athletes. Salaries can exceed a million dollars, and you're covering an area that's a lot of fun. You won't be able to count the number of people who'll tell you they wish they had your job.

Get a Jump on the Job

Get involved in reporting for your school's publication, TV station, or radio station. Learn as much as you can about sports by watching games. Follow your favorite sports writers, sportscasters, and sports shows. Try to analyze what makes a broadcaster successful. Is it his or her knowledge, reputation, delivery, appearance, or catchy expressions?

CARTOONIST

OVERVIEW

While you might think that it would be a breeze to draw cartoons that appear in newspapers or magazines, there's a lot more to the job than you might suspect. Most comic strip animators are self-employed, meaning they have to keep up with the business end of the job while still turning out the necessary cartoons. Although it might seem like it wouldn't be difficult to generate a variety of story lines to accompany the drawings, doing so day in and day out, month after month, can be extremely challenging.

Not all cartoonists generate strip cartoons. There also are political cartoonists, editorial cartoonists, comic book cartoonists, and cartoonists who work for advertising agencies creating cartoons that depict how a commercial or ad will look (called a *storyboard*). The most widely recognized cartoonists, however, are those whose work appears in the newspapers that reach millions of Americans each day. These include Chip Sansom, who pens *The Born Loser*; Scott Adams, who does the *Dilbert* strip; Cathy Guisewite, who writes and draws the *Cathy* comic strip; Jan Eliot, who tells the story of a family in her *Stone Soup* comics; and Bill Schorr, of *The Grizzwells* fame.

These and other cartoonists who create strips use a series of cartoons to relate a joke or tell a story. While some comic strips are simply intended to be amusing, others strive to impart lessons, tell stories, and relate information. Many strip cartoonists choose themes for which they'll

AT A GLANCE

Salary Range

The salary range for cartoonists varies greatly, depending on who buys the cartoons, where they appear, and whether or not you're a syndicated cartoonist. A full-time cartoonist can expect to earn between $24,000 and $48,000 a year on average, although well-known syndicated cartoonists earn much more. Many cartoonists are self-employed and have an additional job or jobs to support their cartooning income.

Education/Experience

Although there are no set educational requirements, a college degree is highly recommended. A degree in the field of art will greatly increase your chances of getting an art-related job, such as an animation artist, which will provide experience that is related to cartooning. In addition, an art education will help to refine and develop your drawing skills. Earning a degree in an area other than art will help you to have a backup plan in the event that you can't support yourself as a cartoonist—at least at first.

Personal Attributes

You'll need to be artistically talented, and you should be able to express yourself clearly when speaking, drawing, or writing. A good sense of humor is essential, as is the ability to manage your time and meet deadlines. You should be self-motivated and able to work on your own.

Requirements

There are no standard requirements in order to be a cartoonist. However, requirements for training, experience, and types of cartoons vary from employer to employer.

Outlook

Jobs for cartoonists are expected to increase by between 10 and 20 percent through 2012. That growth is considered average.

draw and illustrate cartoons for a week or so, then move on to a different theme. Some cartoonists sell their work to just one paper, while others—including all of the better-known cartoonists—get their work syndicated, which means that it appears in multiple papers.

Unless you're very lucky and a syndication service spots your work and decides that every newspaper in the country is going to want to pay to have it included on their pages, getting syndicated requires some intensive effort. You can self-syndi-cate, which means you shop your comic strip around to different editors and hope they agree to run it, or you can look for a syndication service to do that for you.

If a syndication service agrees to take your comic strip and sell it for you, you can expect to pay them between 40 and 50 percent of what you earn from having it appear in the paper. The upside is that being represented by a syndication service means that your comic strip probably will appear in more papers than you could find by yourself.

Jan Eliot, professional cartoonist

Jan Eliot, who writes the syndicated cartoon strip *Stone Soup*, was always interested in art, and her talent was recognized among her peers and teachers in her junior and senior high schools. Although she started her college education in art, she ended up with an English degree.

Ultimately, her art background, coupled with the English degree, turned out to be a great combination for the job she would eventually land with a graphic design agency. Working there, Eliot says, allowed her to combine her abilities in art and writing. "Graphic design was the perfect combination for me," Eliot says.

Yet while she enjoyed working in graphic design, the job just didn't seem creative enough for Eliot. So when a friend told her that she was funny and should consider doing some cartooning, Eliot started thinking about it. "I was frustrated because I felt like I wasn't doing anything that was really creative," Eliot says. "I was thinking that my life was sort of drudgery, and I wanted to find a way to alleviate that. When my friend suggested that I write a comic strip, I thought it sounded like fun."

Her friend offered to serve as Eliot's editor, so that Eliot would be responsible for handing in a comic strip once a week. The problem was, as a single mom with two young daughters, Eliot sometimes found it difficult to meet her deadlines. "I had a lot of ambition, but not much time or discipline," Eliot says.

Nevertheless, still working with the graphic design agency, Eliot began creating cartoons. She'd sell cartoons periodically to a greeting card company, land a contract to illustrate a computer manual or textbook, or find a magazine that would buy one of her cartoons. While she wasn't able to make enough money on the cartoons to support her family, drawing them provided her with a creative outlet and gave her some much-needed experience.

Her first break occurred when her local newspaper agreed to run the comic strip she was creating at the time, called *Sister City*, which tells the story of a single mom raising two daughters—an earlier version of her current *Stone Soup*.

Once you find a newspaper that agrees to run your cartoon, you need to honor your commitment and make sure you finish and turn in your work on time. You won't last long as a cartoonist if you fail to produce what you say you will.

Pitfalls

There are a lot more people longing to be cartoonists than there are cartoon strips in newspapers and magazines. The field is competitive, and even after you break in, it's likely that you won't earn very much

money right away. Moreover, the nature of the job means that once someone has hired you to supply cartoons, you'll face continual deadlines.

Perks

If you enjoy drawing and you're creative and imaginative, you're likely to find that being a cartoonist is extremely enjoyable. Many cartoonists can make their own schedules, working from 9 p.m. until 3 a.m. if they want. Many cartoonists say they didn't choose this career, but simply

Once her cartoon was appearing in the local paper, Eliot began considering the possibility of getting it syndicated. She quickly found out, however, that syndication doesn't happen overnight. Four years and a lot of hard work later, Eliot got lucky. A syndication service liked her cartoon and agreed to help her get it placed in additional papers. Today, *Stone Soup* appears in more than 140 newspapers in six different countries, and is read every day by more than eight million people. "Sometimes it still seems like a dream," Eliot says. "I just can't believe that I get paid to do this."

That's not to say, however, that producing a daily cartoon is easy. She constantly works to come up with engaging story lines and to further develop her characters. Keeping eight million people satisfied every single day causes some significant stress, after all. Eliot says she works 40 hours a week in her home studio, creating and writing story lines and sketching her cartoons.

While her cartoon strip is amusing, Eliot isn't afraid to tackle tough issues such as grief, parenting roles of men and women, dating the second time around, and the insecurities and anxieties of adolescent and teenaged girls. Eliot draws on her own experiences as a single mother for her cartoon strip, which has wide appeal to families of every sort. "Every family has its issues, and I think people appreciate it when someone shares those issues," she says. "I guess *Stone Soup* is a little less sugar-coated than some of the other family strips, and I think people appreciate that."

While a college degree is not necessary to be a cartoonist, Eliot says a fine arts background would be helpful. Regardless of the educational path you take, however, she strongly recommends that you get a backup plan in place. "Even some very successful New York cartoonists had backup careers," Eliot says. "It's not unlike trying to be an actor. You'll probably need to have a lot of jobs waiting tables on the way there."

always found themselves drawing continually from the time they were very young. To be able to make a living from doing something you very much enjoy is satisfying.

Get a Jump on the Job

Get into the habit of carrying a sketch pad along and drawing what you see around you. This will give you good practice in learning to draw accurately, which is important for a cartoonist. If possible, get some art lessons, either individually or in a group setting. Take all the art courses that your school offers, and read any material you can find about getting to be a cartoonist. Practice writing short story lines and illustrating them. If you don't already do so, get into the habit of reading the comics every day. Think about which ones you like most and why. Examine the variety of drawing styles and notice how they differ from one another. Above all, draw as much as you possibly can.

CROSSWORD PUZZLE CREATOR

OVERVIEW

Crossword puzzles must have a tremendous appeal to remain so popular because they ask Americans to do many of the things they often won't do, anymore. Although many of us are in too much of a hurry to sit down and read, we'll spend an hour or longer working on a crossword puzzle. Although many complain that Americans no longer treat the English language with respect, puzzle solvers love the challenge of having their vocabulary tested. At a time when newspapers worry about losing readers to television, the Internet, and technological gadgets, crossword fans continue to dive into their newspapers for the daily crossword puzzle.

Why do crosswords command so much loyalty? It's because their creators, also known as *constructors*, are able to change with the times. Crosswords today barely resemble the puzzles that came on the scene during the 1920s. Obscure and old-fashioned words that once drove puzzle solvers crazy are rarely used in puzzles. While creators still use clues that require you to know your history, they also allow solvers to use their knowledge of today's movies, plays, books, sports, and other areas of American culture. And crosswords aren't just a test of vocabulary. They've become a form of entertainment, too. Many creators and editors—who choose the puzzles that will appear in their newspapers—have

AT A GLANCE

Salary Range
$1,000 to $20,000+

Education/Experience
While you don't need to have a college degree to create crossword puzzles, most creators, also known as constructors, find that education enhances their vocabulary and love of language. Most creators started out by solving crossword puzzles and enjoyed them so much that they started creating their own. Some creators make names for themselves by finishing at or near the top of the annual American Crossword Puzzle Tournament.

Personal Attributes
You should have a feel for entertaining and educating because a crossword puzzle creator does both. You should be disciplined and organized because you'll be expected to meet your publication's deadlines. You should have a sense of humor because you'll want readers to get a kick out of your puzzle's theme and clues.

Requirements
You need a top-notch vocabulary, and it helps to know a little about a lot of things because your clues will come from hundreds of subjects. You'll need to have the computer skills to use software for puzzle makers.

Outlook
Crossword puzzles are here to stay and creating them will always provide part-time work for expert creators. Very few make a living creating crosswords, so this job will remain mainly a labor of love.

enlarged their audience by posting puzzles online.

Most creators are freelancers who don't consider puzzle making a full-time job. They submit crosswords to newspapers, magazines, or news syndicates and get paid anywhere from $35 to $400 a puzzle. Major newspapers often employ crossword puzzle editors, who may construct their own puzzles as well as buy puzzles from freelancers. A successful puzzle should be fresh and interesting, appeal to several age groups, offer a mix of eye-catching words and fun facts, and avoid words that nobody uses anymore. A puzzle's answers may all fit a clever theme, like "vegetable of the day," or may be themeless, which usually makes it more

Stanley Newman, crossword puzzle creator and editor

While still a child in Brooklyn, New York, Stanley Newman solved crossword puzzles in the *New York Daily News* and *TV Guide*. Those puzzles fueled a passion that's stayed with Newman all his life. Even after he became a Wall Street bond analyst, Newman realized he was happier working crossword puzzles. He soon became a crossword champion and, eventually, editor of the *New York Newsday* daily puzzle. That puzzle has become syndicated to more than 100 other papers. "I can't imagine what my life would be like now if crosswords weren't a major part of it," says Newman, who lives in Massapequa Park, New York.

Newman actually didn't realize how much talent he had for solving crosswords until he tried the American Crossword Puzzle Tournament in 1981. "There was no way for me to know I was very good, compared to the rest of the world," he says. "Before I went to my first crossword tournament, I went to a couple of Scrabble tournaments in Brooklyn. I thought I was pretty good [at Scrabble] because I hardly ever lost to most of the people I used to play. But I did miserably, and compared to tournament-level people, I wasn't that good at all. That nearly prevented me from attending my first crossword tournament. I took up competitive crossword solving in the early '80s and that eventually would change my life."

Many might have wondered why on earth Newman would want to change his life. Besides having a good career on Wall Street, he had a bachelor's degree in mathematics from Brooklyn College and a master's in statistics from Rutgers University in New Jersey. Yet he struggled in his first crack at the American Crossword Puzzle Tournament. "I spent the next year training to improve," Newman recalls. "I was the first person who ever prepared for the tournament by serious training and I learned skills that I still retain to this day." Newman defeated 131 other puzzle solvers to win the tournament in 1982. He also was part of a four-member U.S. team who won the 1990 World Crossword Championship. He set a world's record by solving a *New York Times* crossword puzzle in 2 minutes, 14 seconds. And he used his crossword skills to win $112,480 on a TV game show, *The Challengers*, in 1990.

Newman founded the American Crossword Federation in 1983, an organization aimed at making crosswords popular and fun for solvers of all ages. He began editing the *Newsday* puzzle in 1988 and it quickly gained a big following because it emphasized general knowledge and was witty, entertaining, and educational. Although Newman has created more than 1,000 puzzles, he usually creates just one a week for *Newsday*. His other daily puzzles are submitted by freelancers. "I'm glad I don't have to make a new crossword every day because I'd burn

difficult. Good creators don't want readers filling in all the blanks in five minutes, but they don't want them agonizing for hours, either. They try to create a puzzle that's a good challenge yet fun to tackle.

Most constructors are college educated, though there's no single path to this job. Many top creators also write puzzle books and hold seminars to teach fans how to get better at solving puzzles and even create their own. Creators are helped by software, which provides puzzle diagrams, clues, and answers. But puzzle-making software won't automatically make you a

out," Newman says. "The job is intellectually stimulating but it's very challenging. The most enjoyable part is coming up with interesting ideas and fun clues. I very much like clues that paint a mental picture that evoke a pleasant image in your mind. Like for the word 'toe,' there's a very evocative clue—bath water tester. You can picture dipping your toe into bath water. You're not going to find that definition in any dictionary. But it's going to make you smile."

Newman has edited or written more than 100 puzzle books and sponsors an annual cruise on which fans solve and create crosswords. He maintains a Web site, http://www.stanxwords .com, which posts the daily *Newsday* puzzle. "I get one download every second, so I know there are hundreds of thousands of people around the world, from Indonesia to the Philippines to Australia, doing the puzzle," Newman says. "I like to think I'm engaged in a daily mental battle with everyone who does the crossword. I do want everybody to finish, eventually, but I do want them to scratch their heads a little. I don't want people filling in puzzles as fast as they can write."

Newman gives his readers a Sunday puzzle twice the size of the daily puzzle. "The complexity of creating a crossword probably increases geometrically as the size increases," Newman says. "The daily puzzle, from start to finish, takes me about an hour. The Sunday puzzle takes closer to three hours." Newman's signature puzzle is the Saturday Stumper, his most difficult yet most popular crossword. *Newsday* crosswords increase in difficulty from Monday through Friday so that there's a puzzle for most every skill level. The Saturday puzzle is a real stumper because it has no theme, emphasizes longer words over shorter ones, and has tougher clues than appear earlier in the week.

The Saturday Stumpers are so popular that Newman has given hints on solving them during his seminars at the Smithsonian Institution in Washington. "They run a series of classes all year on virtually every subject you can think of," Newman says. "I was flattered to be asked and over 100 people came to my last seminar. It was quite an experience for me." Despite his enthusiastic following, Newman began to worry that some fans assumed that any puzzle with his byline would be just as difficult as the Saturday Stumper. So he started signing his daily puzzles as "Anna Stiga" or "Sally R. Stein," which are anagrams for "Stan again" and "It's really S.N." But his fans got wise to both pen names. They're really the only parts of Newman's puzzles that are easy to figure out.

pro. It's like a tool that can be used more skillfully by a carpenter than by most of us. Though software can create an entire puzzle for even a beginner, it won't be professional enough for any editor to use.

Crossword puzzle creators aren't merely entertaining people these days. According to some researchers, they're improving the nation's mental health. Dr. Gary Small, a neuroscientist at the UCLA Center on Aging, found that crossword puzzles are among the mental exercises that reduce the risk of Alzheimer's. Daily crosswords are considered well suited to maintaining mental agility because they require regular and sustained bursts of brainpower. That's assuming, of course, that you get close to solving them.

Pitfalls

Crossword creators and editors may not always get their fair share of professional respect. Some newspaper bosses may not treat them as serious contributors and pay attention to the puzzle only when readers complain that a clue is missing. Puzzle making pays poorly and very few make a living at it.

Perks

It's very satisfying to know that you're challenging and entertaining your readers. Popular creators enjoy corresponding with fans. The top creators can become puzzle editors for newspapers, teach seminars, and organize social events with crossword themes. Who knows? You may be among the talented few who can make this a full-time job.

Get a Jump on the Job

You can try solving puzzles while you're still in school. Check your local newspaper for puzzles. If you get the urge to create your own puzzles, you can buy one of the many books or software programs available to help. If you think your puzzles are good enough, submit one to your local newspaper. Check out www.cruciverb.com, the popular Web site for constructors.

EDITORIAL WRITER

OVERVIEW

The job of an editorial writer is to provide a voice for a newspaper or magazine. An editorial writer presents and addresses a wide variety of topics, ranging from dwindling farmland or problems within a local government to an emerging school trend or the state's budget.

Unlike reporters who write news stories, editorial writers are expected to express opinions in what they write. The opinion expressed, however, may not be that of the writer. Most papers have editorial boards whose members work together to find a voice that will represent the standards and values of the paper. The person who writes the editorial is expected to reflect the general opinion of the board. Many newspapers, for instance, weighed in on the Terry Schiavo case in 2005, taking a position on whether or not government should have been involved with the decision of whether to remove the feeding tube of the woman who doctors had determined was in a persistent vegetative state.

If the editorial board of a newspaper agreed that the government should indeed have been involved with that decision, the editorial writer would need to echo those views in the piece, regardless of his or her personal views.

Editorial writers are expected to present facts honestly and completely, never basing an opinion or fact on an unknown or a half-truth, and to use those facts to

AT A GLANCE

Salary Range

The average annual salary for a newspaper editorial writer ranges from $22,350 to $47,170, depending on factors such as experience, and the location and size of the paper.

Education/Experience

In the old days, newspaper writing was left to those most capable of tracking down stories, gathering information, and getting it written before deadline. Today, most newspapers won't hire reporters without undergraduate degrees in journalism or mass communications. You'll need to spend a considerable amount of time as a reporter, editor, and columnist before you're assigned to the editorial desk. The position of editorial writer normally is reserved for the most seasoned, experienced staff members who have a thorough understanding of issues of all kinds. For some jobs, employers may require people have degrees in the subject areas they're hired to cover, such as business, health, or science.

Personal Attributes

You should enjoy writing and be able to effectively convey your ideas and opinions. You also need to be comfortable meeting and talking with people from many backgrounds and walks of life, as you will be writing about a great range of topics and meeting a lot of people along the way. You'll need to be able to pick out the pertinent parts of a news story that may lend themselves to an editorial, and be willing to effectively express a viewpoint that you may strongly oppose personally.

Requirements

You'll probably need to be able to drive and have a valid driver's license. If you work for a small paper that doesn't have company cars, having access to a vehicle may also be a requirement. Many employers routinely require drug tests.

(continues)

AT A GLANCE *(continued)*

Outlook

Job growth for all newspaper jobs, including that of editorial writer, is expected to increase by an average of between 3 and 9 percent until 2012. This rate is slower than the average growth rate for all jobs, and is attributed to newspapers merging with others or closing, a decrease in newspaper circulation figures, and less revenue coming to newspapers from advertisers.

draw fair conclusions. They must avoid conflicts of interest, or even the appearance of conflicts of interest. It would be a clear conflict of interest, for instance, if an editorial writer wrote a piece encouraging a municipality to waive zoning laws so that a housing development could be built if the writer stood to benefit in any way from the construction work.

An editorial writer must have an open mind on all topics, and should work at representing different viewpoints and groups in the editorials. As a result, editorial writers are fair game for criticism. Readers frequently respond to editorials by writing letters to the editor, which usually are published on the editorial page, so editorial writers need to be able to withstand criticism.

While editorials usually don't contain bylines (the name of the author), it's easy enough to find out an editorial writer's name by checking the newspaper's Web site. In fact, the Internet may herald a brand new, more interactive editorial approach. Some newspapers have begun posting editorial topics on their Web sites, giving readers a chance to express their ideas and input on different subjects. Proponents believe that allowing readers to interact with editorial writers before the piece is written gives the writer a broader perspective on the topics, and provides facts about which the writer might otherwise not be aware.

Pitfalls

Editorial writing typically is the job of someone who has worked at a newspaper for a significant amount of time, so you'll have to work your way up through the ranks before you'd be eligible for this position. It takes great discipline to come up with ideas, research topics to make sure you've learned everything you can about them, and express opinions that may or may not be your own. Once you've had your say, you can almost be sure that there will be people who disagree with you. And with more and more people relying on sources other than newspapers for information, some believe that the future of newspapers themselves may be in jeopardy.

Perks

Writing editorials can be great fun, especially when you get to express an opinion you share on an issue that's important to you. Editorial writers have the power to influence great numbers of people. You'll meet a lot of people who are influential and involved with your community's decision making, and, because you have to pay close attention to the news, you'll be on top of the issues that affect you and those around you.

James Homan, editorial writer

James Homan writes editorials for a mid-sized newspaper in Reading, Pennsylvania. A long-time employee, he's covered many different beats and shouldered many different responsibilities before being named as one of the paper's two editorial writers. That, Homan says, is typical.

"Editorial writing usually is reserved for someone who has been on a newspaper staff for quite a few years, simply because the longer one has been around, the more familiar he or she should be with the community, its history, and the issues that it faces," he says. That doesn't mean that younger people, such as regular news reporters [called "beat" reporters] don't have valuable input—they do. "Some even develop editorial ideas on their own," Homan says. "But beat writers are supposed to remain impartial, and editorials are supposed to take a stand. So it can be difficult for a beat writer to take an editorial stand and remain impartial."

While Homan enjoys writing editorials, it's sometimes difficult for him and the other members of the newspaper's editorial board to come up with an issue on which they want to take a stand. "It may seem like a simple thing, but if you look at it from a year-long perspective, we have to write 365 editorials every year. That is a lot of opinions," Homan says.

He and other members of the editorial board meet at least once a week to toss around ideas for topics. Once the topics have been determined, they discuss the positions they want to take. Homan is free to express his opinion on any given topic, but once the board reaches a consensus, he's expected to write an editorial that reflects the overall opinion, not his own.

"Many people think that editorials are the opinions of the writers, but they are not," Homan says. "They are the opinions of the newspaper. I agree with some, I disagree with others, but I still have to write them. It's hard writing an editorial with which I don't agree, but that's my job." Once Homan writes a piece, at least three other people read it, checking for whether the facts are accurate and the voice reflects the newspaper's tone.

What Homan enjoys most about writing editorials is the versatility of the work and the fact that the job enables him to meet many different people. "Every day presents a new challenge," he says. "One day I might be writing about township supervisors purchasing a golf course for public use, the next day I might be writing about a cancer-prevention program in the city's school district, and the day after that, it could be the governor's budget. I also get a chance to meet interesting people, many of whom hold very important jobs in business and government."

If you'd like to become an editorial writer, you'll need to be interested and informed on a wide variety of topics, Homan advises, and you'll need to learn to be a good listener. "You never know what you'll be covering, so it helps to have a little bit of knowledge about a lot of subjects, including history, civics, and math. And, of course, you'll need to have good writing ability. But perhaps the most important ability is to be able to ask a question and then really pay attention to the answer. In most cases, the next question will come from the answer to the last question."

Get a Jump on the Job

Read the editorials that appear in your local newspaper, along with those in magazines and larger metropolitan newspapers. Pay close attention to how the writer expresses opinions and draws conclusions. Write for your school paper, and offer to write editorials about topics that affect you and your classmates. Practice writing whenever and however you can, and learn to pay attention to events occurring around you, at the local, regional, state, and national levels. Take any journalism classes your school offers.

FACT CHECKER (MAGAZINES)

OVERVIEW

What's the correct spelling of Kuala Lumpur? How tall is the fence around the White House? Did the director of the Acme Pet Products Company really say what she's quoted as saying?

These questions may sound picky, but that's the job of a fact checker—to identify and verify facts in magazine articles to make sure they're accurate. In the case of quotes, the magazine wants to avoid lawsuits. In the case of Kuala Lumpur, the magazine doesn't want to look stupid.

Finding out the answers to these and many other questions is the job of the magazine fact checker, who uses a wide range of resources such as the telephone, the Internet, and an entire library of reference books.

The best fact checkers are invisible—you never see them behind the scenes, you only see the result of their work: a completely error-free article. For example, fact checkers at magazines such as *People* try to find at least three independent sources for each fact.

As editorial budgets shrink faster than a starlet's waistline, many fact checkers are complaining of being short-staffed and overworked. But they're still retained because having a reliable person check the facts lets the copy editor focus on structure and narrative flow. They're important because mistakes can be costly. Magazines understand that the cost of fighting even one libel suit caused by a mistake could pay for an entire phalanx of fact checkers.

AT A GLANCE

Salary Range
Annual salaries usually range from $21,000 to $35,000 depending on the size of the publication and its location.

Education/Experience
A degree in journalism, English, communications, or similar major is required; some type of broadcasting experience typically helpful. About 450 colleges offer formal programs in journalism and mass communications.

Personal Attributes
Fact checkers should be able to pay extreme attention to detail to the point of pickiness, have a vast store of knowledge, an organized mind, a certain amount of diplomacy, and be able to work accurately and efficiently under deadline pressure.

Requirements
This job usually requires fact checking experience with a magazine or newspaper, and a degree in library science, English, or journalism. Fact checkers also should be familiar with research processes and have excellent written and verbal English skills.

Outlook
Keen competition is expected for many jobs on national magazines located in New York City, because so many people are attracted by the glamour of this industry.

For example, a few years ago a woman's magazine printed an article about decorating wedding cakes and mentioned that lilies of the valley make a nice spring-like decoration. What apparently slipped by the magazine's fact checkers is that lily of the valley is poisonous, and it's one of the last flowers you'd want to drape over anybody's cake. In desperation, the magazine mailed out cards to all its subscribers alerting them to the mistake—at no small cost—but it was impossible to reach all of the potential readers who didn't subscribe.

Fact checking isn't just an important way to avoid expensive lawsuits, but also to guard against those little errors that could damage the public's impression of the publication's accuracy. For example, when one new reporter tossed off a newspaper caption about Queen Elizabeth's ship heading west on the St. Lawrence River—calling it "down river" to Toronto—the newspaper was besieged by bemused readers pointing out that going west on the St. Lawrence is actually "up river." The reporter explained to the irate editor that on a map, the St.

Lawrence river slants downward from east to west—hence, "down river" seemed like a logical guess to a newbie. Had the newspaper used fact checkers, the mistake would never have appeared.

Good fact checkers are always on the lookout for just such problems. Born skeptics, they should have an almost obsessive focus on detail and question just about everything. Most fact checkers are generalists, but some magazines hire fact checkers who are experts in one area, such as health, fashion, history, money, geography, or any other subject the magazine may cover.

The fact checker begins work on each story by carefully reading through the piece

Lori Segal, magazine fact checker

Working in magazines was always the career goal for Lori Segal, who combined journalism classes with her major in American Studies at Brandeis University. After spending time as a college intern working at New York City magazines, as soon as she graduated she began to focus on job-hunting at New York and Boston magazines. After interviewing with several magazines, she applied for a job as an editorial assistant with *Food and Wine*. Although that position was filled, there was an opening in their research department for a fact checker. "They gave me a test, and I discovered I'm a lot more of a detail person than I realized!" she laughs.

Right away, she settled into the fact checking groove at *Food and Wine*, and liked what she was doing. "It was kind of intense," she recalls, "and a little more academic," which she liked, having so recently left the academic world. But after checking facts for a while, she realized she was ready for something different. "I decided to try the other side [of magazine journalism], and I worked for a woman's college doing their alumni magazine." That experience made her realize she really preferred working for popular magazines.

"I knew I wanted to work at a woman's magazine," she says, "and I knew I liked women's issues." When a job opened in the research department at *Cosmogirl!*, she snapped it up.

As associate research editor there, Segal's job is to check each and every article to make sure all of the information is correct. "Basically, any story we get—whether it's a fashion article, a celebrity interview, an entertainment piece, or something about beauty or health, I go through and fact check." That might mean contacting physicians to check facts if it's a health article. A piece on fashion might require her to make sure the magazine has all the right information about details and price. Entertainment pieces entail contacting publicists to make sure the details about TV or movie stars are correct. A big part of her job is checking information via LexisNexis, the Web, and dial-up online searchable database with access to more than 3 billion documents from

and checking each fact and quote. Some magazines require writers to provide their notes featuring the written quotes or tapes of quotes; others simply ask for contact information. These magazines then call up the individual and read the quote to ensure accuracy. Combing even a short piece to check on names, ages, dates, locations, and other details can take at least a day—and that's if everyone you call is available.

Pitfalls

Fact checking can put the individual in an uncomfortable situation and requires a lot of tact and diplomacy, because although you're trying to help a writer, you're really challenging their version of the truth. Some writers will become hostile when facts are questioned. It can also be quite tedious; it may take days to wade through three paragraphs in a 5,000-word piece.

Perks

People who do well in this job love information and, even more, love getting to the truth. They typically prefer working alone and finding things out, and for a true fact-hound, being a fact checker is simply a lot of fun. Working for large metropolitan magazines also can be fun and glamorous, although the job itself may not bring a lot of prestige.

thousands of sources. "I always check facts against the [interview] transcripts, or I might call someone and check the factual information in a quote," she says.

Segal advises prospective fact checkers to spend time in school doing research—especially working with Lexis at school. Getting a couple of internships while in college is also important. If you snag an internship at a magazine, "say you'd love to help out with fact checking," she says. "That's good to put on your resume. Also, as you read through magazine articles, think about what they had to go through to check this. Think about how you'd check facts."

In general, Segal really loves her job. The only downside, she says, is when a writer is guilty of poor reporting. "Sometimes it's very frustrating to get an article at the last minute and there's a lot of incorrect information and they leave it for the fact checker to fix," she says. Her favorite writers are those who provide lots of good backup and get their information correct the first time.

Although employees in the New York magazine world are notorious for job hopping from one magazine to the next, fact checkers tend to be a more stable lot. "People in research tend to be a little bit longer term than some other positions," she says.

For her, she's living her dream job. "Especially at the entry level, when you're doing research you're dealing with content a lot more than you usually might, " she says. "And you're dealing with the top editors, and learning a lot. All that information is great at cocktail parties," she laughs, "but unfortunately it only stays in your head about three months."

When she first started out, Segal says she assumed that a job in magazine research might be a stepping-stone to something else, perhaps an editor position. "But now I really want to make a career of it," she says. "I really like it. There's a lot of contact with different editors, different people. It's not so isolating in this department. There's something different every day."

Get a Jump on the Job

If you're pursuing a career in magazines, you should probably get some initial experience working as an intern at a magazine. Although these positions are usually unpaid, they sometimes provide college credit or tuition. More importantly, they provide hands-on experience and a competitive edge when applying for jobs. In this highly competitive industry, magazines are less willing to provide on-the-job training and instead seek candidates who can perform the job immediately.

FOREIGN CORRESPONDENT

OVERVIEW

No job in journalism has a more glamorous ring to it than "foreign correspondent." People imagine a world of intrigue, danger, and excitement. They imagine interviews with shadowy figures in dark corners of cafes, and think of a foreign correspondent as an eyewitness to history.

Although there's some truth to these stereotypes, when you come right down to it, foreign correspondents are just newspaper reporters working overseas. Once the novelty of being abroad wears off, reporters find the same challenges and practice the same skills that they did back home.

Foreign correspondents have long held an important place in American journalism, and they're even more important now. Historically, because the U.S. borders only two other nations and sits oceans away from most of the world's news centers, most Americans in the 20th century barely noticed the rest of the world except during wartime. Today, we can't afford to ignore the development of a global economy, the impact of international financial markets, the threat of nuclear weapons and terrorism, and the grim realities of genocide and epidemics. It's the job of the foreign correspondent to bring these stories home and help us understand how events overseas affect Americans.

Most foreign correspondents are veteran reporters. They've covered important local and national stories for newspapers at home, or worked in the Washington,

AT A GLANCE

Salary Range
$40,000 to $120,000+

Education/Experience
You'll need a college degree, preferably in journalism or another communications major. Foreign language and international studies will come in handy. Before you're considered for a foreign assignment, you'll have to prove yourself as a top reporter, preferably at the national level.

Personal Attributes
You should enjoy (or at least be able to tolerate) constant travel. You must be open-minded enough to realize that people in other nations may view the world much differently than you, and you've got to be able to adjust to unfamiliar food, time zones, languages, and customs. You should be curious about other countries and be willing to study their politics, economics, history, religion, and culture.

Requirements
You should speak one or two foreign languages, although you might not use them as much as you'd expect. You'll need computer skills and the technological know-how to transmit stories from almost anywhere. And you'll need a U.S. passport and any visas required by nations in which you'll be working.

Outlook
Fewer U.S. newspapers are hiring their own foreign correspondents. Most papers are owned by chains with foreign news bureaus that provide stories to all papers in their chain. Many newspapers keep costs down by getting foreign news from wire services. As some parts of the world become more dangerous for U.S. journalists, fewer papers and chains will put their correspondents in harm's way. There will be intense competition among top reporters for the foreign jobs that become available.

D.C., bureau of a major newspaper or newspaper chain. Many wrangled a foreign assignment by improving their credentials, going back to school and studying foreign languages and international issues. In most cases, overseas assignments usually are voluntary—but highly competitive. Experienced reporters often view foreign work as the chance to tackle a new challenge and grow professionally. They're usually assigned to a foreign capital or other major city, and from there, they travel throughout the country and perhaps to bordering countries, too.

Correspondents quickly learn that it's harder to break big stories overseas than back home. That's because they're trying to beat other journalists on their own turf. Just imagine a French correspondent moving to Washington and trying to compete with

Matt Schofield, foreign correspondent

Whether he's reporting in the United States or in Europe, Matt Schofield, European bureau chief for Knight Ridder, is always on the lookout for unusual stories. His stories don't get much stranger than the one about a Romanian who attacked a corpse that he believed to be a vampire. The man was arrested for disturbing the dead, then protested his innocence to reporters while neighbors in his small town listened. "This was one of the most interesting stories I've worked on, just for the 'Wow, this is a different type of moment,' " Schofield recalls. "We held an open bar for an entire town—the bill was $15—and heard the lament of the vampire killer. He says, 'Why is this a crime? If he was already dead, then who did I harm? But if he was a vampire, I saved my family.' "

Schofield wasn't taught about vampires when he took a break from reporting at the *Kansas City Star* in 2001 to attend Harvard University on a Nieman Fellowship for a year. Instead, he learned about the European Union, which raised his interest in working overseas. After completing his fellowship, he volunteered to cover the invasion of Iraq for Knight Ridder Newspapers. He also covered the start of Iraq's reconstruction and guerilla insurgency. "It was fascinating, if a bit frightening," Schofield says. "I had a series of meetings, and many cups of tea, which culminated in a fairly lavish lunch with one of the Fallujah sheiks. He was intelligent, thoughtful, a charming host, and he was coming from a completely different perspective on Iraq than any American I'd met. At the end of the meal, he apologized for not being able to show me his hometown, as the security was a bit difficult at the moment. When he left, an assistant of his leaned over and explained, 'We're very sorry, Mr. Schofield, but if we were to bring you into Fallujah just now, it is very likely that you would be kidnapped and killed.' "

Schofield became Knight Ridder's European bureau chief in 2004. He was based in Berlin and covered all of Europe with the help of just one office manager and a staff of stringers. He became responsible for 40 countries and had to be on top of such varied stories as terrorist attacks on the London subway, German elections, and meetings of the World Bank, International Monetary Fund, and European Union.

"The biggest change in the job from what I've done before is the size of the territory," Schofield says. "Even when I was working for a national desk in the States, we didn't cover all of the nation. In this job, I do cover all of Europe. Source development isn't so much about all the U.S. newspaper, radio, television, and Internet reporters who've spent years developing sources in the U.S. government. That's why correspondents often concentrate on follow-up stories that explain to readers back home how foreign news may affect them. While a Saudi reporter may break a story about an increase in the price of oil, a foreign correspondent may focus on how this increase will affect motorists in the United States and U.S. relations with the Middle East.

A foreign correspondent must constantly pay attention to the foreign media, especially when a big story breaks. He or she also must attend meetings and ceremonies that are big news back home. When an international conference on global warming is finished for the day, key participants usually meet with the international news

working the beat as it is about figuring out the underlying themes that unite what's going on in different countries. You don't often work with the same sources on a daily basis. On sources, there is occasional overlap. The terror experts you deal with on the Madrid bombings can help you out on the London bombings and on terrorism-related stories in general. These sources, however, don't have a lot to say about the Orange Revolution in Kiev, or the collapse of the European Union, or vampires in Romania. As with all reporting jobs, there's a good mix in the type of sources we use. When something huge breaks, it's not uncommon to hear about it on the BBC, or from one of the dozens of people I work with around Europe. I keep an eye on competing media [from the United States], but a far closer eye on non-competing media, especially the national newspapers throughout the continent."

Anyone who hears Schofield describe some of the places he's visited and big stories he's covered might be dazzled by how glamorous his job sounds. But that's really the Hollywood image of a foreign correspondent. "It's not a glamorous job," he says. "It's still newspaper work. It's not the movie—hanging out with the gang in cafes, scribbling stories on the backs of napkins and tying them to the legs of pigeons before throwing on the trench coat and heading off to overthrow the Third Reich. But it's the best gig I can imagine in the business. I have such incredible access to events that change the world. That's where the professional fulfillment comes in, and for me, at least, it was difficult to get at home.

"The most enjoyable part of the job is seeing new stuff. Even in the cities I think I'm getting used to—Paris and Rome and London and Athens—there's always something amazing to learn each visit. But for those hoping to do this, prepare to spend insane amounts of time on your own, trying to figure out new places. It's exciting but it gets to some people." Language barriers are not as much of a problem as you might think. Although Schofield speaks French and German, he's always worried that even a slight misunderstanding by him could distort a source's quote. "I've been in 27 countries since I started this job and have not spoken a word of the language in most of them," he says. "Even with languages I do speak, I prefer to work through translators. I've done interviews in both languages but I'm always nervous about them. Speaking the language is an advantage, but not a huge one."

Breaking news speaks a language of its own.

media, and translators are present to bridge the language barrier. The U.S. delegation may hold a separate news conference to accommodate U.S. reporters. Perhaps a correspondent knows somebody in the U.S. delegation who will provide additional information or quotes that competitors won't get. Then it's time for the correspondent to get back to the laptop computer and write a story, which will appear in the next morning's newspaper and probably on the paper's Web site. Foreign correspondents help make the world a smaller place.

Pitfalls

You're usually working alone, so you don't have other staffers filling in when you need a day off. Trying to stay on top of the news of an entire country or continent can be tiring and stressful, as can be the travel. You may get back home only a few weeks a year, so this is no job for those who easily become homesick. Correspondents with children may have to pay expensive tuition at private schools for international students.

Perks

You'll see parts of the world you've never seen, and you'll reach a new level of professional respect and fulfillment. Once you've done a good job as a foreign correspondent, you'll probably be able to write your own ticket in journalism when you return home. And who knows? Maybe your experiences will give you material for a best-selling book.

Get a Jump on the Job

Study a foreign language or two. Stay on top of international news from newspapers, magazines, radio, television, and the Internet. Travel abroad if you can. See if your school sponsors a student exchange program or an overseas trip. If you're in New York, visit the headquarters of the United Nations and sit in on a session.

GOSSIP COLUMNIST

OVERVIEW

Gossip columnists make a living doing what everybody else does for free. People have the irresistible urge to spill the beans—or "dish"—about their friends, enemies, relatives, or anybody else. The richer and more famous the person, the juicier the gossip, and nobody generates more gossip than a movie star or another major celebrity. We see newspaper columns, supermarket tabloids, magazines, TV shows, and Web sites devoted to celebrity gossip. A provocative outfit worn by an actress at the Academy Awards will generate more coverage than the latest bill passed by Congress. An entire industry of photographers, known as the paparazzi, has sprouted up to satisfy the public's insatiable demand for candid photos of celebrities. Most gossip columnists have no shortage of material or readers.

If you're a gossip columnist, the type of publication that hires you and the standards of your community will determine how far you can push the envelope. Some gossip columnists are allowed to report any flimsy rumor if it's hot enough. But others are held to the same rules for accuracy as any other reporter or columnist at their paper. Some papers consider gossip as their bread and butter. Tabloids like the *New York Post* aggressively promote their gossip columns. They usually have three columnists who fill an entire page of gossip. Other papers consider the tabloids too bold but hire gossip columnists to satisfy readers who want something juicier than

straight news about the celebrity scene. Even distinguished papers like the *New York Times* and *Washington Post* have

AT A GLANCE

Salary Range
$30,000 to $1,000,000+

Education/Experience
You'll find gossip columnists who don't have college degrees or traditional journalism backgrounds, but you're better off with a degree, preferably in journalism or another communications major. Gossip columnists may be hired from the reporting ranks or they may come from fields like music or film, where they've made contacts that will help them cover the celebrity-driven world of gossip.

Personal Attributes
You need to enjoy being out and about because clubs and social events are some of your best places for finding gossip news. You must be outgoing and comfortable schmoozing with all kinds of people. A gossip columnist doesn't have to be the life of the party but shouldn't be a wallflower, either. You must be an aggressive reporter because most people don't want you nosing around in their business. You'll need a thick skin to handle complaints from people who think you've embarrassed them.

Requirements
You'll need a clear, lively, and breezy writing style. You'll need to have the pulse of your city's celebrity scene. You'll need to know the people your readers want to know about and know the sources who can tell you about those people.

Outlook
Gossip is a growth industry. Every news outlet devotes time or space to the lives and times of celebrities. As long as there are celebrities with devoted fans, there will be jobs for gossip columnists.

gossip columnists. The most popular gossip columnists are handsomely paid. When Liz Smith, then 82, had a highly publicized contract dispute with her employer, *Newsday*, her income was reported to exceed $1 million a year.

A gossip columnist in most markets is the only staffer on the celebrity watch. But in a big city with a big celebrity scene, you'll need a staff to help you collect all the juicy gossip. In New York, Los Angeles, or Washington, D.C., a gossip columnist would be run ragged trying to attend every party, opening night, or club likely to attract celebrities. That's why *New York Post* gossip columnists have two full-time

Hearne Christopher Jr., gossip columnist

Hearne Christopher Jr. has an unusual background for a journalist but just the right background for a gossip columnist. He was a commodities trader, rock promoter, and alternative newspaper editor and writer before Jim Hale, publisher of the *Kansas City Star*, asked Christopher if he'd like to cover the city's celebrity scene. Christopher had lived in Kansas City all his life and his previous jobs made him familiar with the area's business and political leaders and the club, concert, and arts scene. After struggling to find a format he liked, he developed a strong following for his column. "I think it's more of a guerilla force of journalism because in the daily paper most of the time, the regular reporting can be stodgy or restricted because of the standards," Christopher says. "It's good to attain those ethical standards but a lot of things don't come out. It's like putting a Spam filter on your Internet. If the filter's really strong, some good stuff will get filtered out in the process."

Gossip columnists in mid-sized markets like Kansas City must be more resourceful than those in major cities. Los Angeles has film stars all over the place. Washington, D.C., has all the nation's major political figures and an endless social calendar. New York is the nation's media capital, home to the major television networks and publishing houses. It's also a major performing arts center and has countless celebrities living there or just passing through. So a business executive who'd fly below the social radar in New York might be a regular in Christopher's column. "We don't have Madonna or Britney Spears coming through town," he says. "Occasionally, you'll have Christina Aguilera being finicky about her dinner on the Plaza (a popular shopping and dining district). But I look at the column as a sitcom with local people who are willing to play the game. Most people don't want to play the game of being candid and out there. So the column becomes a rotating cast of regulars. When *Friends* started, nobody knew who the actors were. But once people started watching them, they became interesting to all the viewers."

Many aren't happy to wind up in Christopher's column. Members of an exclusive private club became upset when he reported that exotic dancers were hired to carry the ring cards at the club's ballroom boxing show. An official of a parochial boys high school told a *Star* editor that Christopher invented his quote about pranks being played on campus by students from a sister school. Christopher, though, had the quote on tape. He's become accustomed to sources

assistants each. The *New York Times* gossip columnist has two assistants plus stringers. Items should be verified and a tip may require hours of follow-up calls. Richard Johnson of the *New York Post* once was sitting in a restaurant when a stranger came over and handed him a sheet with a juicy gossip item about her company. But

don't hold your breath waiting for that kind of help. You'll be wearing out a lot of shoe leather to collect your items.

You may be surprised to learn that gossip columnists also get a lot of items from celebrities' publicists. Many actors and actresses, especially those still trying to get noticed, find it helpful to get their names in

claiming they were misquoted or taken out of context, especially when an item gets them in hot water. "I have a term for that," Christopher says. "I call it 'source remorse.'" Then there are the people who won't talk to him in the first place. During his early days at the *Star*, Christopher couldn't get a certain lawyer to return his phone calls. It turned out the lawyer assumed the calls were a friend's idea of a joke. "That was my first hint that people feared a call from Hearne Christopher," the columnist says. "I found it astounding that a gossip column was such a foreboding deal. He was certain he would get thrown under a gossip bus."

Christopher gets into areas other than celebrity watching. He'll often break stories about local businesses opening and closing or, perhaps, being run by shady characters. He'll also hang out the town's dirty laundry. When Christopher learned that the owner of an infamous X-rated bookstore had died, he wondered why the death hadn't been reported. He found that the owner's obituary had, indeed, been published but mentioned only his military service and good deeds. Christopher made sure to give readers the rest of the obituary. He'll also weigh in on hot political issues. When Kansas City debated whether to replace its old arena, those in favor of a new downtown arena claimed it would attract a lot more concerts than the old one. Christopher used his experience and contacts as a rock promoter to show that was not the case.

Promoting concerts and trading commodities was an odd combination of jobs. Christopher went to work for the family brokerage firm, B.C. Christopher, after he dropped out of the University of Arizona. When the firm was being sold in the 1980s, a local business publication kept writing error-filled stories speculating about the sale. Christopher realized the errors resulted, in part, from the firm's refusal to comment on rumors. "I stepped in and I'd call back to explain everything and I was able to dilute the sensationalized stuff," he says. "That's what gave me insight into dealing with journalists—being on the tortured side of the phone."

His concert promotions got Christopher involved with a record store owner who also owned *The Pitch*, a publication mainly to promote the store. Christopher offered to sell ads and hire writers for *The Pitch*. He built a popular weekly for concert fans, but *The Pitch* was going broke. Christopher became involved in the sale of the paper and in 1992 approached Jim Hale to see if the *Kansas City Star* would buy them. Hale had no interest in the paper, but a lot of interest in hiring a gossip columnist, which is how Christopher lost a sale and found a job.

a high-profile gossip column. Others find it annoying and even insulting. For celebrities, gossip columns are double-edged swords. For you, it might be an enjoyable and challenging way to use the pen.

Pitfalls

People who don't like what you've written about them may threaten to sue you or complain to your boss. You may have to wrestle with your editor to keep an item in your column that might be considered too bold. You'll put in long hours and, if you're married, spend a lot of evenings away from your family.

Perks

You'll get paid for being at clubs and parties. You'll meet a lot of interesting people from show business, the arts, and business. You'll have a lot of flexibility in picking your topics and deciding where to hang out. If you're a top gossip columnist, you'll have assistants and an excellent salary.

Get a Jump on the Job

Become familiar with reporting and the celebrity scene. Get as much reporting experience as you can on school publications. Keep up with the celebrity scene by going to the movies and concerts and listening to contemporary music. Observe how the celebrity scene is covered by your local newspaper, supermarket tabloids, and entertainment shows on television. Which type of celebrity reporting do you find most interesting and entertaining?

HELICOPTER NEWS REPORTER

OVERVIEW

Helicopter news reporting entered a brave new world on June 17, 1994. Former football star O.J. Simpson was about to be arrested on murder charges when he jumped in his Ford Bronco, driven by friend A.C. Cowlings, and led police on a low-speed chase on Los Angeles area freeways. A bizarre scene unfolded, with onlookers on overpasses cheering Simpson and a fleet of news helicopters following the Bronco. Viewers around the nation couldn't take their eyes off their TV screens. Helicopters had been used all the time for radio and TV traffic reports, but now they were suddenly important players in hard news coverage. It wasn't long before every TV news station in the nation owned or leased a helicopter. Advances in technology soon were allowing TV stations to get their pictures clearly and immediately from helicopters.

The Bronco chase showed the value of helicopters for news coverage. When news breaks, a reporter and camera operator can hop in a helicopter and quickly be in the air and headed to a news scene. Helicopters can use small areas for take-offs and landings and reporters don't have to worry about traffic jams, one-way streets, or trying to peer through fences. Helicopters can provide live shots of crime scenes, police chases, natural disasters, and any other event best observed from a bird's-eye view. They can also increase

AT A GLANCE

Salary Range
$50,000 to $100,000+

Education/Experience
You should have a college degree, preferably in journalism or another communications major. You need just as much training for reporting in the air as on the ground. If you're also the pilot of a news helicopter, you'll be expected to have at least a few hundred hours of flight time under your belt.

Personal Attributes
You'll have to be a fast responder. When news breaks, you'll need to be in the air within five minutes and ready to cover a story. You'll also need to be adventuresome, especially if you're a storm chaser. And you'll need to be highly competitive because every helicopter team wants to be on the scene of the story first.

Requirements
You should be reasonably fit physically and comfortable in the air, especially when you hit turbulence. If you're piloting a news helicopter, you'll need the appropriate license.

Outlook
Helicopter coverage will continue to be a standard part of television and radio news. The number of jobs for helicopter news pilots and reporters should remain stable.

the number of events a reporter can cover in a day. Some stations, for instance, use helicopters to take sports reporters and camera operators to all the important high school football games in one metropolitan area on a Friday night.

Some helicopter pilots double as reporters, although you don't find many people that versatile. Most stations have a pilot on call and assign a reporter to hop in the helicopter. The pilots usually are self-employed or work for companies that lease helicopters to stations. The most popular helicopter news reporters on radio and TV usually cover rush hour traffic. They hover over congested roads and warn viewers and listeners about accidents, delays, and incoming storms. They're equipped with a scanner to monitor emergency channels that announce traffic accidents.

Helicopter reporters also have become valuable in covering weather, especially

Johnny Rowlands, helicopter news reporter

Viewers and listeners in metropolitan Kansas City know pilot and reporter Johnny Rowlands best for his morning traffic reports, but what really gets his juices flowing is the chance to respond to breaking news. Rowlands had just finished his morning traffic report and was sitting in his office at the Johnson County Executive Airport in May 2005, when a friend phoned to say it looked as though a bank up the street was being robbed. A Channel 9 producer soon called Rowlands to tell him that the alleged robbers were leading police on a chase in his direction. Rowlands and cameraman Robert Cross were soon in the air. "I have the helicopter set up like a fire engine," Rowlands says. "I can get up in three minutes and I'll be flying 100 miles an hour." He heard police sirens and the next thing Rowlands knew, the alleged robber and several hostages were speeding in a van to the airport. The robber got out of the van and at gunpoint tried to hijack a plane from a flight instructor and student who were preparing for takeoff. Police shot the robber but mistakenly suspected the men in the plane were accomplices who were there to help him escape. Police forced the instructor to the ground and handcuffed him. Rowlands knew the instructor, Matt Miller, and said on the air, "Unless this friend of mine has been leading a secret life, no way he had anything to do with this."

Miller was Rowlands' sidekick when he became a radio traffic reporter in 1983. "I only had 300 hours, so I had him fly with me for the first six months because I was scared to death," Rowlands says. "I knew I didn't have the experience and [bad] weather can get you killed faster than anything. You always have to remember, 'It's fun, but don't forget it can kill you.' I've only had two mechanical failures, one relatively minor and one major." Rowlands' helicopter once experienced hydraulic failure, which is akin to losing power steering in a car. But he was near an airport and able to get down and skid to a stop. Rowlands' biggest scare came during his early days of storm chasing when a fuel control failure caused his engine to run too fast. "You lose all control and it's equivalent to being in a blender," he recalled. "The way the helicopter was shaking, I thought it was going to come apart. It was the scariest it's ever been in the air. I cut off the fuel supply [to kill the engine]. I didn't think we'd make it to the ground, but it stayed together and we landed in a farmer's field."

Rowlands' workdays seldom are that exciting. He's usually helping motorists avoid delays and warning people about severe weather. Rowlands has been groomed for this work since he was a preschooler. "I was born with the flying gene and the weather gene," he says, laughing. "I've loved airplanes ever since I can remember. I took flying lessons when I was 16 and got an airplane license to fly just for fun. I wanted to fly for the airlines but my vision was not good

severe storms. Known as "storm trackers," they fly near approaching storms to judge their ferocity and get video of damaged areas. This helps viewers prepare for hurricanes, tornadoes, and other dangerous storms. A storm-chasing team needs a pilot who can keep a helicopter out of danger and a reporter with a knowledge of meteorology. Members of a helicopter news teams are often a station's stars. Perhaps you've seen TV stations run ads in which a reporter comes leaping out of a

enough. When I was five, my best friend and I started WBW, for 'World's Best Weather.' We would announce the weather on my dad's loudspeaker. When I was eight, I started the Breezy Heights Weather Service. There were about 30 houses on a horseshoe-shaped block and I'd type up the weather forecast and put it in people's mailboxes. Then in high school, some friends and I started the Kansas City Amateur Weather Service. We were all weather geeks."

Rowlands graduated from Baker University in Kansas in 1973 with a degree in communications and a minor in journalism. He was a disc jockey for Baker's radio station and after graduation became a professional disc jockey for 10 years. But playing tunes didn't fulfill him. So he lobbied his station, KMBZ, for a traffic reporter's job, which he performed at first in a small plane. "I always thought it would be cool to combine the two things I like to do," he says, referring to flying and reporting. "I thought traffic was radio at its best—real-time information that people can take action on. As far as the immediacy of it, that's why there's been an explosion of helicopter coverage on TV. If we can show a tornado and give very specific information that can allow people to take action and avoid getting hurt...there's nothing that feels any better in life than helping someone else. And it's just as important to tell them everything's O.K. as that something's bad."

Rowlands likes to consult with Channel 9 meteorologists to help him better understand storms. Not that understanding traffic reporting is all that simple. Many of the accident reports he initially hears on his scanner are inaccurate, so his producer verifies them by calling police dispatchers. "About 75 percent of the time when you get a report of an overturned semi, it's not true," Rowlands says. "Anybody can read a list of traffic accidents, but I don't want people to have to interpret what they mean. They want to know, 'Tell me what effect this is going to have on me.' I have some very strong philosophies on how to report traffic. I am an educator. If traffic is moving 60 miles an hour and you have an accident and traffic's stopped, it's backing up at a mile a minute. If somebody's still home, I can tell them to allow for a 10-minute delay. If rain is expected, I can tell them to anticipate accidents and get an early start. And it's just as important for people to know when traffic is cleared as when the problem started."

Rowlands takes pride in providing news, traffic, and weather coverage that's complete and immediate. "The most important thing is to get there first," he says. "If you get the reputation of arriving first, the perception will be that this station is where you can see what's going on. You have to work hard. Hustle is everything. I'm doing what I like. I'm flying a helicopter, looking down at people's houses and they're watching me. There's a little absurdity to that."

helicopter, with a microphone in hand and a camera operator close behind, to give the lowdown on a breaking news story. If you like reporting and you like to fly, that newsperson could be you.

Pitfalls

This isn't a job for late sleepers. If you're doing the morning traffic report, you'll have to be in the air for the start of rush hour about 6 a.m. You'll also run the same risks, such as turbulence and crashes, as anybody who flies every day.

Perks

For people who enjoy flying and reporting, this job offers the best of both worlds. It really gets the adrenaline flowing to jump in a helicopter and try to beat your competition to breaking news. Helicopter news reporters consider their job a lot of fun.

Get a Jump on the Job

You can start honing your reporting skills at your high school or college newspaper or yearbook. Many colleges offer journalism programs that include live reporting assignments. If you want to join the hardy band of pilot/reporters, you'll need flying experience, either in the military or through private lessons.

HOROSCOPE COLUMNIST

OVERVIEW

Planning a trip, making some money, or getting ready to meet a tall handsome stranger? If you want to see what the immediate future has in store, you can find it all in a newspaper or magazine's daily or monthly horoscope. Sometimes dismissed as a lightweight, superficial type of astrology by more traditional astrologers, horoscope columns can be a steady source of income for astrologers who can write and meet deadlines.

After all, who hasn't eagerly opened the newspaper at some point and searched for their astrological sign to find out what the day will bring? Horoscope columns are in fact not really a stepchild of more "respectable" astrological charts, but are based on the ancient practice of augury—figuring out the best time to do a certain thing. Even modern princesses and presidents' wives are said to have consulted astrologers to discover the best time to plan certain events. This is also what newspaper horoscope writers do—they decipher the movement of the planets and how it might affect a person's actions or life themes.

A horoscope writer studies a wide variety of planetary cycles, blending and interpreting their effects. Of course, horoscope columns—which rely only on the *birth sign* or *sun sign* (the position of the sun on the day you were born)—ignore the moon and rising signs. This produces a simplistic view of a person's chart that only reveals a small part of the story.

Still, if you've ever had a fight with your best friend and then read that very prediction in your daily horoscope, you've seen evidence of the astrologer's ability to interpret specific messages and trust his or her interpretations. This ability to trust your intuition comes with practice.

AT A GLANCE

Salary Range

A columnist can expect to earn between $10,000 to $30,000+, although well-known syndicated columnists earn much more. The salary range for horoscope columnists varies greatly, depending on who buys the column, where it appears, and whether or not you're syndicated. Many columnists are self-employed and have an additional job to support their income.

Education/Experience

While no specific degree is required, casting a sun sign horoscope requires basic experience in astrology, which can take years to master.

Personal Attributes

Horoscope writers should pay great attention to detail, and have lots of empathy, intuition, and the ability to meet deadlines.

Requirements

You'll need excellent writing ability and the ability to understand and apply astrological concepts in order to churn out weekly or monthly horoscopes.

Outlook

Fair. There are a limited number of outlets for horoscope columns in newspapers and magazines. Most astrologers also write books and make the most of their income by private consultations.

Most newspaper astrologers have spent years in self-study learning about astrology and how to cast birth charts. In order to come up with a horoscope, astrologers get their basic facts from ordinary astrology charts. Then, following guidelines that are part of elementary astrology (such as which planets rule which sign) and using astrological symbols, the astrologer interprets this information and writes out the daily, weekly, or monthly horoscope. Modern day computer programs can make short work of the mathematical calculations that used to be required.

So why would two different astrologers come up with two different interpretations for the same sign on the same day? Most readers don't realize that horoscope information is interpretive. For example, two meteorologists could take the very same weather data and interpret it in different ways, based on their own experiences with the way weather usually works. In much the same way, many astrologers have been

Jodie Forrest, horoscope columnist

By the time she was just eight years old, North Carolina astrologer Jodie Forrest had started to read astrology books. Bitten by the astrology bug at such a young age, she gobbled up all of the available texts she could find.

"I could cast charts with about 75 percent accuracy by the time I was in junior high school," she says. "I just figured it out on my own by extrapolating between the date ranges given in the books I was reading. I was doing informal readings for friends by the time I was in high school."

When she met her future husband Steven, an accomplished North Carolina astrologer himself, he showed her how to do the math and how to use the extra tools she needed to cast horoscopes accurately. "I realized it could be a career when I met Steven, who was doing it full time," she says. The two of them began working on astrology together.

"The best thing about being an astrologer is that I can set my own hours, I'm my own boss," she says. "It's intellectually and creatively challenging, and it helps people." But the fact that people find it so helpful can also cause problems—there's a high demand for the work she does. "There is a high risk of burnout," she says. "When you work at home, you also live at work, and you have to be very careful to create separations between home and work life. Because I'm introverted, intense work one-on-one with people can be draining. I have to monitor my energy carefully, and make sure I do things that refresh me and put gasoline back in my tanks, too, so to speak."

Because it's so challenging for Forrest to work directly with her clients, the part of astrology that she truly enjoys is writing astrology columns. "I just plain love to write," she says, although she notes that she also finds writing an astrology column frustrating, because there is so much more to astrology than sun signs. "Just looking at how the planets are affecting each sun sign every month is very much on the surface of what astrology can actually do," she says. "We all have a lot more in charts besides the sun!"

She published a monthly forecast for each sun sign for *South* magazine, which wanted a contemporary Southern spin on the column. "Since I was born in Virginia and have lived most of

trained in the same traditions, but they interpret what they see differently—that's why horoscope columns are different but still may sometimes discuss the same general themes on the same day.

A good horoscope in the newspaper gives you enough specific details that you can apply it to your situation, but is also general enough so it can apply to many different people. You make the column meaningful to yourself by the way you interpret what you read.

Pitfalls

No matter how good an astrologer you are, it can be tough starting in this business. Getting a column syndicated, or even picked up in your local paper, can be extremely difficult.

Perks

Astrologers usually do what they do because they love the work and they enjoy writing. It is enormously fulfilling to see

my life in the South, 'pitching it Southern' was easy and fun," she says. "To make it technically correct, although far more superficial than what astrology can do, I studied the planetary motions for that month and how they would affect each separate Sun sign, and made the forecast accordingly."

Writer's block has never been a problem for her. "Writing is easiest for me," she says. "I love to do it and, apart from length specifications, it's utterly under my control. I also love coaching students one on one about how to do readings and set up their practices. It's very gratifying to see students progress, and to see people using the readings to help themselves."

In addition to the horoscope column, Forrest also writes astrology books and fiction, and produces astrology reports, tapes, and CDs. She also gives lectures and private readings.

If you have a yen to write a horoscope column, Forrest advises that it's important to first understand yourself as well as possible, or you will project your own unresolved issues into the horoscope. "If getting some therapy doesn't feel appropriate, then read M. Scott Peck, John Bradshaw, Melody Beattie, Melanie Klein, Alice Miller, Milton Erickson, Virginia Satir, or Jean Bolen."

It's also important to learn how to write and communicate succinctly and well, and to adapt your vocabulary level to the newspaper or magazine's reading level. "Read lots of fairy tales and fables and mythology, which are all fertile sources for stories you can use to illustrate your readings," she says. "Try Carl Jung, Marie-Louise von Franz, Bruno Bettelheim, Joseph Campbell, and Clarissa Pinkola Estes." She also recommends that budding horoscope writers read a lot of horoscopes from astrologers with different styles. "You'll learn a lot, and also decide what type of astrology or presentation does and doesn't work for you."

It also helps if you have an agent who can help you negotiate rates, she says. "Let local magazines know you'd be interested in doing a column, after you've written up some good samples. Set your rates according to the market and your experience level."

your work in print, especially if you're successful enough to get picked up by a syndicate. It can also boost your credibility and help improve your bottom line as you branch out into books, workshops, or private consultations.

Get a Jump on the Job

Since there are no prerequisites for this career, you can start as early as high school to learn the complex, ancient basics of astrology. There's a lot of math and astronomy involved, so bone up on those subjects, too. Read as much as you can, and if possible, have your natal chart cast by a reputable astrologer so you can see what's involved. Talk to professional astrologers or horoscope writers about their careers and listen carefully to any advice.

HUMOR COLUMNIST

OVERVIEW

There's nothing funny about the state of humor writing these days. Once upon a time, some of the nation's best-known journalists, such as Russell Baker, Art Buchwald, and Erma Bombeck, were humor columnists. These days, the newspaper spaces that once brought us humor are often filled with cranky political commentary. Isn't there room for a few laughs anymore? There is, but you have to look harder than ever to find them. Many newspapers cut costs by using syndicated or freelance humor columnists instead of hiring their own.

You really need a gift and passion for writing humor to make a living at it. Dave Barry has had a fabulous career showcasing his humor in newspapers, novels, public appearances, and his Web log. But newspapers seldom conduct talent searches for humor columnists. Usually, editors will spot a staff reporter who shows a flair for humorous writing and will give him or her the chance to write a column. If the column catches on, the humorist may be sought for radio and television appearances and even have the column syndicated. Successful humorists usually have collections of their columns published in a book and juggle paid speaking engagements.

The most popular humor deals with family life. Political humor can be amusing but readers seem to get the biggest kick out of columns that make them laugh about common, everyday experiences. Most humor columnists get their best material

AT A GLANCE

Salary Range
$2,500 to $100,000+

Education/Experience
You'll need a college degree, although you won't be able to major in being funny. Shoot for a degree in journalism, English, or anything else that will develop your writing. A lot of humor columnists start out as reporters, then get a chance to try humor when their editors notice they have a flair for witty writing.

Personal Attributes
Although you don't have to be a gifted comedian, you must be able to view the world from a different—and funnier—perspective than most people. You'll need to be disciplined because you'll have to write your column even on days when you don't feel especially funny.

Requirements
You must have a clear, compact, and punchy writing style. Readers won't be amused by long and clumsy sentences. Although you're not required to have a family, it's difficult to write humor without one. Humor columnists often rely upon their spouses and kids for column material. If you don't have a family, how about starting with a pet?

Outlook
This is not one of journalism's growth areas. Fewer and fewer newspapers are hiring full-time humor columnists. But if you have good ideas and your writing is clever, you can find a paper that will appreciate your sense of humor.

from kids and spouses, especially their own. They write about the baby crying in church, the stressed out mom in the mall, the weird behavior by the bride's relatives at a wedding, or whatever prize the cat drags in. Where most people see problems and embarrassment, the humor columnist sees another act in the human comedy. He or she is able to look at the world from an uncommon viewpoint. Readers who might've screamed or cried over a personal mishap often get a good laugh reading about a columnist suffering that same kind of mishap. It always seems funnier when it happens to somebody else.

But humor columnists don't always have funny ideas drop into their laps. Weeks might pass without a columnist having car problems, illnesses at home, a fight with a spouse, or an incinerated burger. So

Jared Fiel, humor columnist

Jared Fiel's career as a humor columnist for two Colorado newspapers would've been a success if he made only one reader laugh. That would be Tracy Hume, who enjoyed Fiel's columns so much that she married him. Hume lost her job in Sacramento, California, in 1990 and moved back home to Fort Morgan, a small town where she figured she was doomed to spinsterhood. Hume liked to read *The Fort Morgan Times* and in 1992 noticed that Fiel, pronounced "File," was writing a humor column called "Fiel's Files." The couple met while Hume was freelancing for the *Times* as a high school football reporter, and their love story was chronicled by the *Ladies Home Journal*. Tracy has also become Fiel's editor and a regular character in his columns.

"She had grown up in Fort Morgan, a small town, and she had the sensibilities of the community. Sometimes, I was writing things that probably weren't the best for a small town. And sometimes when you start riffing in your head, it's really funny but it doesn't quite read the way it's in your head. I always say my columns are a lot funnier before she gets to them. When we had kids, that's pretty much been the source of humor in my life," Fiel says. "When my kids were young, our two-year-old son was sitting in the middle of the garden and chewing on a bunch of rocks and my wife, who's the ultimate germ-a-phobe, totally freaked out. So I took the rocks away and he started screaming. And she looked at me like I'd screwed up again. She took the rocks, put them in the dishwasher and gave them back to my son to eat. I said, 'This is absolutely insane,' and there's my column. Every minor life incident in the last 10 years has been in the newspaper. But we celebrated our 11th wedding anniversary, so we're surviving."

The couple moved to Greeley and Fiel became a freelance humor columnist for the *Greeley Tribune, Fort Morgan Times* and *Rocky Mountain Parent Magazine* while he worked as marketing director for Aims Community College in Greeley. He started writing humor at small newspapers in California and New Mexico after getting a push in the right direction from a professor at California State University, Chico. "We were writing a play about a guy about to get married and one of my professors said, 'You ought to be writing humor columns,'" Fiel recalls. That turned out to be good advice, except the professor forgot to tell Fiel about the difficulty of finding good column ideas.

"Reading people who you find funny helps a lot," he says. "Watching comedians, that plays a huge part, too. You don't use their style but you realize they're looking at the world in a

what's the idea-hungry humorist to do? Most humor writers watch the late-night talk show hosts, cable comedy shows, and even the political news. You never know when one joke or news event will trigger a column idea. Getting the idea is just the first step, though. Then you have to make

it read funny. And even if the column seems funny to you, how do you know if your readers will laugh? Stand-up comics can check out the mood of a live audience and adjust their routines as they go along. But if readers are groaning instead of laughing at the first paragraph, there's no turning

totally different way and that's what makes them funny. You realize that you have the same set of eyes as they do and can look at things in a way where, instead of getting ticked off, you can say, 'This is pretty darn funny.' If I have a fight with my wife, in the back of my head I think, 'This is a great column.'"

Fiel's columns about his wife and two sons get the best response from readers. His book, *Fumbling Thru Fatherhood*, is a collection of his columns. "You can write about the funny things the government does and they just don't connect the way the personal stories do," Fiel says. "The columns I always get the comments on—when people stop me in the stores—it's always the kid ones. The average newspaper reader is 55 years old and they love to read the kid stories. They love to watch other parents suffer. Everybody's gone through all that. It also connects with parents going through that right now. My dad's taken more heat in my column than anybody because I've compared my fumbling through fatherhood to his, and he says, 'Everybody in Colorado must think I'm an idiot.' " Maybe not, although Fiel's readers tend to remember what he writes.

"The greatest experience for anybody who writes is to have your stuff quoted back to you," he says. "I absolutely love it when a column connects with people. I have people who actually cut things out that I've written and send me a little note about their kids and how the same thing happened to them. When you get a column that really clicks with people, it's so fun. They flip to your column and their day is funny. They get a laugh and to me that means more than anything. One lady was suffering from cancer and would have her nurse read her the column and said that was the only laugh she had all day. How do you beat that?"

Because he writes for small communities, Fiel bumps into his readers a lot more often than do most humor columnists. That's a mixed blessing, because most strangers expect him to be funny. "If somebody comes up to me in the grocery store, you feel some sort of pressure," he says. "Some people just stare at you, like, 'Okay, be funny, funny boy.' Am I supposed to grab the oranges and juggle? At parties, my wife gets the occasional comment that her husband must be so funny at home. She says, 'Yeah, he *thinks* he's funny.' I have friends and relatives who are leery about being in the paper. Something will happen at a party and they'll say, 'You're not going to print this, are you?'" Not unless it's really funny.

back for the humor columnist. Even the cleverest writers know they can't always leave them laughing. Some days, leaving them with a smile will have to suffice.

Pitfalls

People may try to avoid you in public for fear their behavior will land them a spot in your column. You may feel pressured to write something funny on days when you don't feel like being funny. Jobs are becoming scarcer for full-time humor columnists.

Perks

The job's a blast, especially when you know you've given somebody a good laugh to help them through the day. It's nice to get calls or e-mails from appreciative readers. Top humor columnists can increase their fun and income through books, speaking engagements, and even scripts for plays and films.

Get a Jump on the Job

Who do you think is funny? Check out the late-night talk show hosts, famous comedians, and humor columnists. Consider their styles and material and why they can make people laugh. Once you get a feel for good comedy and effective writing, you can start to develop your own style of humor.

INVESTIGATIVE REPORTER

OVERVIEW

Many in the news business consider the term *investigative reporter* to be redundant. After all, isn't all reporting investigative? Do you really need to give somebody a specific title before they're qualified to investigate corruption, waste, and incompetence? But for want of a better term, reporters who dig up the stories that are hardest to uncover became known as investigative reporters. That term gained a new popularity when Bob Woodward and Carl Bernstein of the *Washington Post* broke a series of stories exposing the Watergate scandal.

The stories began with a June 1972 break-in of Democratic National Committee headquarters at the Watergate hotel and office complex in Washington, D.C. This was five months before Richard Nixon was re-elected president with a landslide victory over George McGovern. The *Post* reported that one of the burglars was a security aide for the Nixon re-election committee. More stories by the *Post* and other newspapers and an FBI investigation revealed that Nixon campaign officials had ordered the break-in. Nixon and his aides tried in vain to cover up their involvement and Nixon resigned from office in August 1974. Woodward and Bernstein won a Pulitzer Prize for their coverage and wrote a book, *All the President's Men*, which became a movie. As a result, being an investigative reporter seemed like one of the most glamorous media jobs in America.

AT A GLANCE

Salary Range
$35,000 to $100,000+

Education/Experience
An undergraduate degree, preferably in journalism, is a must. You'll have to prove yourself as an aggressive reporter on daily stories before you're assigned to investigative projects. Any background in accounting or law is valuable because financial and legal documents will be important to your research.

Personal Attributes
You'll have to be tenacious because you'll be digging for hard-to-get information. Although you sometimes may be part of a reporting team, you'll often be on your own for long stretches and may feel lonesome. You must be thick-skinned when you talk to people who don't want to answer your questions or won't answer them truthfully. And you'll need to be friendly and trustworthy to gain the trust of those who are willing to help you.

Requirements
You must have writing skills that enable you to make complicated matters clear to most readers. You must be willing to protect the identity of a confidential source, even if it means you could go to jail.

Outlook
As newspapers and broadcast media keep cutting expenses, there will be fewer investigative reporters who get several months to work on a major project. Reporters now often are expected to write and research investigative stories in addition to their daily responsibilities. While the number of jobs for investigative reporters should remain stable, there will be less time to work on investigations.

Hardly anybody starts out as an investigative reporter. Most new reporters begin by cranking out daily stories on a specific beat, writing heartwarming feature stories, expressing opinions, or exposing wrongdoing. Reporters who are willing to plow through often-confrontational interviews, complicated documents, and many dead ends are good candidates for investigative reporting. However, few ever get their

teeth into a story as juicy as Watergate. Yet Woodward and Bernstein used the same tools and skills that would be used to expose corruption in your local housing agency or mayor's office. They recognized an important story, found the right sources, and studied the right evidence. The story

Tim Weiner, investigative reporter

Tim Weiner won a Pulitzer Prize in 1988 for his series of reports in the *Philadelphia Inquirer* on the Pentagon's "black budget." This was a huge secret fund used to build weapons and finance intelligence work. Although a Pulitzer is considered a reporter's ultimate prize, Weiner didn't really do anything for his "black budget" series that he hadn't done before. The series proved bigger than most of his other stories, but his methods remained the same. "It's the job of the investigative reporter to find those inconvenient facts that are hidden," says Weiner, who moved to the *New York Times* in 1993. "They're not in front of your nose. They're not just lying on the table for you to pick up and they're not available at a press conference. They are beneath the surface of things."

So how do you get beneath the surface? You have to understand the workings of a company, government agency, criminal organization, or whatever else you may be investigating. You have to trace the flow of money. And you have to study the history of the people or organizations you're investigating. "You have to develop a core knowledge about the way things really work," Weiner says. "Take the lid off and look at the machine inside. How do you do that? First, you have to devote yourself to learning the basic mechanics of the system you're studying. How does a bill become a law? How does a case proceed to trial? How does a building get built?

"And you have to understand how money flows. If you want to understand how a city or police department works, you have to understand the money. No matter what your beat is, you have to understand the budget because money is power. You have to understand the language of your beat. If you're talking to somebody at the Pentagon, your bank, or your school, you have to talk to them in their language. You have to understand how things have worked in the past. History is your only road map to the future."

Perhaps the toughest part of investigative reporting is getting information from people who may not want to get involved with a story that's going to raise a stink and possibly get them fired. "Whether you're dealing with the cops or the CIA, you get the information by winning the trust of the people you are dealing with," Weiner says. "If they don't trust you, forget about it."

Weiner used all these basics to research and write the story that won him a Pulitzer Prize. "I was interested in how the Pentagon was able to build weapons in secret," he says. "As anyone who read the paper would've known, there were certain huge programs—like the B-2 bomber—that were being constructed in secret and their costs were hidden. There were wild estimates of what was being spent—$30 billion or $40 billion—and nobody really knew. So I sat down with

may have gone nowhere had Woodward and Bernstein thought they were covering a routine burglary.

Once they discovered the burglars had ties to Nixon campaign officials, one revelation led to another. Woodward and Bernstein had many helpful sources but none more valuable than W. Mark Felt, the second highest-ranking FBI official. He was known only as "Deep Throat" until he revealed himself in 2005. Woodward was a young Navy lieutenant carrying documents into the White House when he accidentally met Felt and struck up a

the Pentagon's budget, which is broken into four broad categories of spending, the two most important of which are research and development and procurement. Each program is broken down into a line item. If you added up all the line items that were public and unclassified and then looked at the bottom line, you could see that there was a gap. Many billions of dollars. I tracked that back over the '80s. Each year's budget took a day to add up because there were thousands of line items. You could see that the secret portion of the Pentagon budget was deleted because the items were either given a blank space, a phony code name or were disguised as something else. This secret portion had quadrupled during the Reagan administration [1981-1988] and there was 36 billion dollars, give or take, for both secret weapons and covert operations."

Weiner then asked public officials if they could explain or justify the Pentagon's secret budget. "Armed with this knowledge, you could go to people on the Hill and in the defense industry and say, 'What is going on here?' " Weiner says. "The general feeling was that things had gotten out of control. As I finished my interviews, the whole Iran-Contra thing exploded." The Iran-Contra scandal revealed that Reagan administration officials had been selling arms to Iran, a U.S. enemy, in hopes that Iran would help free U.S. hostages being held by terrorists in Lebanon. The money received for arms was then sent to the Contras, anti-Communist guerillas in Nicaragua. Both activities violated stated administration policy and legislation passed by Congress. They also raised the issue of whether spending not approved by Congress had gone too far. "So you had a political context, as well as a military context, to define a phenomenon of secrecy gone wild, which made people more willing to speak," Weiner says. "There's a point where secrecy becomes undemocratic and this was the feeling among both Republicans and Democrats in Congress, as well as some dissenting voices in the Pentagon. That got me interested in covering the CIA, which I did for the next decade."

Winning a Pulitzer, certainly, helped Weiner get to cover what he wanted. "It was very nice, but the reward is in the work," he says. "If you set out to win that, it's self-defeating. It's not the Nobel Peace Prize. It doesn't make you a better reporter. In fact, these awards sometimes paralyze people because they think every story they write has to be a Pulitzer Prize winner. There's a large element of luck. The real award you have to work for is the sense that you can help right wrongs. Sometimes you can put the bad guys in jail. Sometimes you can raise public awareness of injustice. Sometimes you can enhance the public's right to know. Our role is not to win prizes. Our role is to serve as a check on the abuse of power."

conversation. They stayed in touch and Felt offered Woodward career advice. He later gave Woodward vital clues to tracking one of the most important stories in the history of American journalism. Good reporters stay in touch with their sources.

Felt's famous advice to Woodward was, "Follow the money." He meant that Woodward should study the cash flowing in and out of the Committee to Re-Elect the President. Some was used to finance the burglary. Most scandals are exposed by financial documents. Corporate corruption, illegal drug rings and scandals in military spending, foreign aid or illegal campaign contributions usually can be uncovered by financial documents. They show how money is spent, hidden or stolen.

That's why investigative reporters spend weeks, months, and even years studying documents and conducting interviews before they get to the bottom of an important story. Some projects require so much work that a team of reporters will be assigned to them. The work can be difficult, lonesome, and sometimes even boring. But when a long investigation finally turns into a front-page story and commands the attention of the entire nation, and maybe the world, an investigative reporter's time and effort will seem worthwhile.

Pitfalls

You'll get frustrated when you go days or weeks without important information.

Reporters who like to see their bylines every day may not enjoy waiting long stretches to see their stories published. You could be called as a witness in a criminal investigation.

Perks

You'll get tremendous satisfaction when a powerful investigative story opens the eyes of readers and makes your community and nation more honest and better governed. By exposing crimes in high places, you might help those in lower places. The Enron scandal not only ruined a company, but put thousands of people out of work and wiped out much of their savings. That scandal wasn't exposed in time to help its victims, but the scandal you uncover might be a different story.

Get a Jump on the Job

Join your school newspaper and learn the basics of reporting. Apply for a summer internship with a local newspaper or radio or TV station. Believe it or not, you can learn about reporting by studying your school's gossip mill. How much of the gossip turns out to be accurate? Which of your friends is the most reliable source? Ask yourself if you've been careful enough evaluating the information you get and if you've been asking the right questions. Then you'll be thinking like a reporter instead of a rumormonger.

MAGAZINE EDITOR

OVERVIEW

Magazine editors are responsible for the editorial content of their magazines. They read, revise, rewrite, and edit copy written by staff members, freelance writers, guest writers, and others, making sure the copy is accurate and error free. Depending on the structure of the magazine and the size of the staff, an editor also may be responsible for generating and assigning stories. Some editors write a regular column, or contribute articles to the magazine.

A large magazine has many editors, each of whom plays a different and specialized role. There is an executive editor, who oversees assistant editors with varying duties and assignments, and normally has the final say on how stories are handled. A managing editor handles the daily operations, while assignment editors make sure there are writers available to cover all the stories and articles that must be written. Copy editors read and edit copy to make sure it meets the standards of the magazine. Smaller magazines may have fewer layers of editors, meaning that one person has to assume the duties of several jobs at a larger publication.

It's important for a magazine editor to know both his or her staff and the magazine's audience. You need to know what sort of articles your readers are looking for and make sure they're written in an interesting and informative manner. Knowing your staff enables you to match writers with the stories to which they're best

AT A GLANCE

Salary Range

Salaries range from $24,010 to $76,620, with an average salary of $41,170.

Education/Experience

You'll need a college degree to get a job as a magazine editor, preferably in an area such as communications, English, or journalism. If you want to work for a specific type of magazine, such as a health magazine, a concentration in a health-related subject would be useful. If you want to work for a food magazine, some culinary training may be necessary. If you have your heart set on editing a science magazine, take as many science courses as possible.

Personal Attributes

A magazine editor must be prepared to deal with the unexpected and be resourceful and flexible. Publishing is not an exact science. A writer gets sick or injured and can't get a story turned in on time. A source suddenly becomes unavailable and you've got to scramble to find another one. An editor has to be ready to change gears and do whatever is necessary to get the work done and the magazine to the printer—perfect and on time. As a magazine editor, you'll need to be able to express yourself well and convey ideas. You should be curious, and knowledgeable about a wide range of topics. You'll need to have good judgment concerning what and how material is presented, and display a strong ethical sense. You should be creative, persistent, able to stand your ground, and able to work well with others.

Requirements

Requirements will vary depending on the employer.

Outlook

Jobs for magazine editors are expected to increase at an average rate of between 10 and 20 percent through 2012. Additional opportunities may become available with the increase of online magazines.

Jeffrey Mervis, magazine editor

Jeffrey Mervis is an editor at *Science* magazine, an international science journal based in Washington, D.C. His basic responsibilities include writing, editing, and researching science stories, which involves a significant amount of interviewing. He also works with staff writers to assure that their work meets the standards of the magazine and to assist them with their assignments.

Although his college degree is a bachelor's of science in history, Mervis has always had a keen interest in the areas of science and mathematics. His writing career started almost accidentally during his senior year of college.

"I took one writing course in college during my senior year," Mervis says. "I was lucky enough to have an essay I wrote be published in the college alumni magazine. Seeing my byline in print was a real thrill."

Driven by a strong interest in current events, Mervis landed a job after graduating from college with a small, weekly community newspaper. He interviewed people and wrote stories, took photos and even laid out the copy. His next job was with a small, daily newspaper in Ohio, from which he was able to move to a large city paper in Washington, D.C.

When that newspaper shut down, Mervis was hired as the editor of the monthly newspaper of the American Psychological Association (APA), which rekindled his interest in science—and 25 years later, he still is fascinated.

"I started to interview scientists and write about what they do as part of my job with the APA," Mervis says. "I've been doing it for almost 25 years now, including the last 12 years at *Science*."

Even though his job at *Science* includes many duties other than interviewing scientists and writing about what they do, it's still Mervis' favorite part of the job.

"I love having the opportunity to meet and talk to smart and interesting people who are doing fascinating things," he says. "Scientists love to talk about their research, and most enjoy explaining what they do to people who aren't scientists."

The most difficult part of writing or editing scientific copy, he says, is assuring that a complex and difficult topic is explained clearly, in language that the average reader will be able to understand. And, Mervis says, although it's tempting sometimes to pretend you understand something when you really don't, it's not a good idea.

"It's a challenge to admit that you don't understand something. But you have to be willing to ask scientists to explain their work in everyday language. If you don't understand it, your readers won't, either," Mervis says.

Mervis advised anyone interested in being a magazine editor to read and write as much as possible about a wide variety of topics. Pay attention to current events, he says, and know what's happening in the world. And, he says, don't be afraid to ask questions when you don't understand something, or simply if you're curious.

"The job of a magazine or newspaper editor is to find and write up news that people will want to read," Mervis says. "So, the more you know, the more you'll be able to tell your readers."

suited. If one of the writers used to work in the medical field, for instance, it probably makes sense to assign him or her to a health-related story.

Editing a magazine can be stressful since you're working to meet ongoing deadlines. You must be able to manage people and be supportive of others who are also working under stressful conditions.

Most large magazines are concentrated in major cities, such as New York, Boston, Philadelphia, Chicago, Los Angeles, and San Francisco. Smaller magazines, however, are based all over the country.

A magazine editor is essential in assuring that the publication's content meets the standards of the organization. Editors also may be responsible for hiring writers, reviewing and following up on readers' responses to published material, and making sure work is completed in a timely manner.

Pitfalls

Editing can be stressful work, there's no question about it. Not only are you working with writers who are under pressure, but you're working to meet deadlines and challenges of your own. If you're looking for a five-days-a-week, eight-hours-a-day job scenario, being a magazine editor probably isn't a job you'd like. You need to be able to plan far in advance, which

can be difficult and stressful, and you also may be pressured by financial constraints if advertising revenues drop.

Perks

If you like a job that changes constantly, offering new and different challenges on a daily basis, you may do well as a magazine editor. People who work at magazines tend to be well-informed and interesting, which makes the working environment interesting and energizing. Chances are that you'll meet or at least learn about interesting people who are featured in or interviewed for stories.

Get a Jump on the Job

Get as much writing experience as you can by volunteering for your school newspaper and looking for other writing opportunities. Do you belong to a religious group or other organization that publishes a newsletter? Offer to write an article that's relevant to teens. As you get older, look for writing internships. Some newspapers contain special sections for teens that are printed on a regular basis. Any sort of writing experience you get will be beneficial. Learn to read with an eye to editing. Scour your school and local papers and mark any mistakes you find. Mistakes happen, and it's the job of an editor to find and fix them.

MOVIE CRITIC

OVERVIEW

Movie critics get paid to watch movies and review them for their audience. It sounds like a job that just about anyone could do, but in fact, it's a highly specialized career that requires a lot of background and cinematic knowledge. Some movie critics are syndicated, which means their reviews appear in multiple publications.

Movie critics also must work hard to leave their personal biases outside the theater door and be as objective as possible. When you review a movie, you have to be able to see it on different levels—it's not just about whether or not you like the film. Many movie critics will watch the film more than once before they actually write their review.

The first time through, a critic will simply watch the film and experience the feelings it evokes. The second and perhaps even third time, the critic will analyze technical factors such as the screen composition, direction, the body language of the actors and actresses, and the camera work involved. It's this technical analysis that sets the movie critic apart from the vast number of movie fans who watch a show for entertainment. Someone who doesn't have training in film would be able to experience the movie, but wouldn't have the expertise necessary to appreciate the technical aspects and direction of the film. That requires a deeper understanding of the industry. Understanding the ins and outs of film allows good reviewers

AT A GLANCE

Salary Range

Salaries for movie critics vary tremendously, depending on who employs the critic, how well known he or she is, and other factors. There are many movie critics employed by newspapers, whose jobs include tasks in addition to reviewing movies. A movie critic working for a mid-sized newspaper can expect to earn between $32,000 and $53,000 a year, depending on how long he or she has worked there, job performance, and other factors. A full-time, celebrity movie critic would earn much more.

Education/Experience

Movie critics must be knowledgeable about all aspects of film. You'll need a college degree, preferably in English, journalism, broadcasting, theater, or another area of liberal arts. Make sure you take plenty of classes in art, film, photography, and psychology. Some critics earn an English or journalism degree, and then get a master's of fine arts in film or a related subject. Take elective courses about the movie industry, because you'll need an understanding of film history to write effective reviews. Many movie critics are hired as freelancers, which means they submit film reviews without being employed by the publication for which they're written. Others are employed by a newspaper, magazine, or online publication.

Personal Attributes

You'll need to be able to think objectively and express yourself clearly. You also need to be task oriented and able to complete deadlines on time. You should be able to work under stressful conditions and willing to put in the time necessary to complete a job.

Requirements

Requirements will vary from employer to employer.

(continues)

AT A GLANCE (continued)

Outlook

The outlook for newspapers is not a rosy one, and, as a result, jobs for movie critics in that venue are expected to increase at a rate that is lower than average—only 3 to 9 percent through 2012. Newspapers are struggling with decreasing circulation and advertising profits and increasing expenses. As a result, many are closing, merging, or consolidating. However, there are more and more films being made all the time and an increasing number of online reviews, which could temper the dwindling number of print jobs.

to articulate why they liked or disliked a movie.

In addition, a movie critic needs to have a historical perspective concerning film, and understand the psychology involved in making movies.

The classic film *It's a Wonderful Life*, for instance, was almost universally panned when it was released in 1946. Just emerging from World War II, American audiences at that time were looking for happy, feel-good movies, not a dark film about a man seeking purpose in his life and not finding it.

Today, however, the movie is aptly appreciated and is considered one of the great American films.

Whether or not an audience will like a movie depends on various factors, including the political and psychological climates of the time. Movies can serve as diversions in time of stress, teach lessons, or expose societal problems. The job of a movie reviewer is to recognize the context of the movie in the greater framework of society, and be able to tell the purpose it serves.

Pitfalls

Jobs for movie reviewers are not as plentiful as, say, jobs for waiters or accountants. Most movie reviewers rely on income from other endeavors to supplement the money they earn watching movies and writing reviews. Some might teach film courses, while others rely on additional writing jobs. It's not impossible, but it's difficult to make a living reviewing movies.

Perks

If you love film, and most movie critics do, it's a great job. Film critics sometimes receive perks, such as free passes and refreshments. Major cities are the sites of film screenings, where critics are invited to come to review a just-released movie. What's not to like about getting paid to watch movies, except maybe when they're really bad? Movie critics always have something to talk about, and often become celebrities in the areas in which they live. You'll always find people who want to get your opinion on a particular film.

Get a Jump on the Job

See as many movies as you can. Renting them works equally well as seeing them in the theater. Try to pay attention to how the camera moves, how the actors relate to one other, and other factors that you may not have noticed before. But don't just watch movies—read as much as you can about movies, including serious books about the industry, as well as all the movie reviews you can find, paying attention to what it contains and how it is presented. Volunteer to review movies for your school or community newspaper, or try out for an internship. Read to get a historical perspective on movies and how they've helped to shape America's culture.

George Hatza, Jr., movie critic

George Hatza, Jr., a movie critic for a mid-sized paper in Pennsylvania, has been reviewing film for nearly 30 years. He is the newspaper's entertainment editor as well as a movie critic, so he wears many hats and has many responsibilities. Reviewing movies is one aspect of his job that he thoroughly enjoys.

With an educational background in English, art history, and stage directing, Hatza says he is qualified to review TV, film, and theater, each of which is very different from the other and requires different skills.

"Every art medium is different and has to be reviewed differently," Hatza says. "I can't review music because I don't know enough about it. With my background in art history I could review art if I had to. But theater, film, and TV are the areas I'm most comfortable with."

Hatza, who has taught film at the college level, knows what to look for when he's reviewing a movie. He understands how films are directed, and how to watch for techniques and actor performance.

"Everything that happens in a movie means something," Hatza says. "No piece of a movie is haphazard."

Hatza also recognizes the tricks filmmakers sometimes use to manipulate viewers into feeling a certain way. While he is aware of those tricks, even Hatza sometimes feels himself getting pulled into a movie and losing his objectivity concerning the film. "I can see the trick, but sometimes it really works. In those instances, you just have to excuse it and accept that whatever technique the filmmaker used was effective."

While Hatza has his own ideas of what makes a good movie, he is respectful of fellow movie critics.

"It's still amazing to me that I can read one review and think the reviewer must have seen a different movie from what I did. And then I'll read another review and find out that reviewer saw the movie exactly the way I did. It's really mind boggling."

In addition to working on being a good writer, Hatza advises anyone interested in being a movie critic to learn to think analytically, and to explore and understand how the creative process occurs. It's not enough just to know whether or not you like a movie.

"Good critics are able to explain why they did or didn't like a film," Hatza says.

Hatza predicts that we will begin to see an influx of movies dealing with different cultures as we struggle to understand a world that is much different from us.

"That's what I'd start thinking about and looking for," he says. "We're learning that we don't live on an island, but that we live in the world. Maybe these types of movies can begin the process of our opening our eyes and minds and hearts to people who are different from us."

NATIONAL GEOGRAPHIC PHOTOGRAPHER

OVERVIEW

Few jobs on earth carry the same cachet as those magic words: *National Geographic* photographer—a job classification synonymous with daring, skill, talent, patience, hard work, nerve, and artistry. Although at any one time there are more than 50 freelance photobugs all over the world snapping away for the *Geographic*, only about five are actually staffers with full-time credentials. These staff photographers are all extremely experienced photographer stars, with acres of credits, lots of books, and plenty of exhibits under their belts.

As a freelance photographer who works for *National Geographic*, you'll typically come up with your own assignment ideas and try to sell them to your editors. If you're successful at convincing them your idea has legs, you'll get the assignment. Some photographers hear about stories that are being planned, and they request it. If you want to get a story approved, you'll do a "one pager"—a single page explaining why you think the story is important, what's unique about it, and why the *National Geographic* should spend the money to cover it. If you're approved—the work really starts!

Once you've gotten the okay, you'll need to start your research and create a general list of situations to photograph. You can spend weeks and even months

AT A GLANCE

Salary Range
About $80,000 to $100,000 a year for a freelance photographer, including side assignments and marketing of your own work. The U.S. day rate is about $400 to $500.

Education/Experience
A solid education and degree in photojournalism or photography is important, as are courses in languages, sociology, and anthropology—plus a lot of photography experience. Most *Geographic* photographers started out as newspaper photographers. *National Geographic* looks for photographers who understand the idea behind the magazine's photography, which falls somewhere between literal newspaper photography and the stylistic approach of photographs in a gallery.

Personal Attributes
Photographers for the *National Geographic* must have patience, tact, excellent oral communication skills, and be willing and able travelers.

Requirements
You have to be able to see with an eye of an artist, and you have to have a point of view, as well as terrific photography skills and an entrepreneurial spirit. You also need to understand what *National Geographic* is looking for—photos that tell a story in a more compelling way than a newspaper but that are more journalistic than a gallery photo exhibit.

Outlook
Who wouldn't want to work for *National Geographic*? Keen competition is a given for photo spots at this magazine, because so many people are attracted by the glamour of this position. You'll have the best chance if you have a college degree in photojournalism or photography as well as many years of relevant high-quality work experience.

doing research on your subject—many photographers say they spend as much time in research before they go out on a shoot as they do on the shoot itself. All of this research can help you figure out what kind of shots you're going to go after. Once you're in the field, you need to work hard at discovering what it is you want to say photographically. When you look into a viewfinder, you're looking at your truth,

Scott Sroka, *National Geographic* photographer

Scott Sroka was in high school when he was bitten by the photography bug. "The school's audiovisual guy, Vic Chamberlain, set up a darkroom in a back office of the library for a group of students interested in learning the process of developing and printing their own photos," he says. "I remember the impact of watching those black and white prints develop, especially the almost bigger-than-life 11-by-14s."

From then on, his career path was set. A fine arts major in college, Sroka worked in commercial art after graduation and later moved to Washington, D.C. There, he began working as a freelance photo assistant. It was, he says, "an excellent way to see how professionals work and learn about the real world of photography—sometimes the hard way!" The job involved a lot of travel, planning, thinking, and heavy lifting. "It not only taught me a lot about lighting and cameras, it also allowed me to meet a lot of interesting people—often in interesting settings."

But of course, being in Washington, D.C., Sroka had always thought the *National Geographic* was the ultimate place for a photographer. "I knew a few people who worked in their educational department," he says, "so I applied in their photo archive and was offered a job based on my hands-on knowledge of photography." He worked for several years as a researcher and photo selector for the new electronic database of images they were creating—no more heavy lifting!

Eventually, he got tired of looking at all those great photographs while he was sitting at a desk, and went back to freelancing. Since then, he's been creating images (both art and photography) in locations from Florida to Alaska, across the Southwest United States, and along Route 66, for a wide range of clients—including some promotional photo shoots for National Geographic Television.

On one occasion, *Geographic* editors needed some images of herpetologist Brady Barr for an ad in the magazine, and the deadline was close. "I got a call asking if I could meet him at this spot in the middle of Everglades National Park and take some photos of him catching alligators—in the dark—tonight!" At this point, Sroka was living in Florida, about a three-hour drive from the Everglades. "I managed to get there and meet him... The late afternoon light was great, with big puffy thunderclouds. At first, the gators were tiny two-footers. I had [Barr] holding them out toward the camera, like posing someone with a small fish.

"As it got darker, they got bigger and bigger. There was a nearly full moon low in the sky, but our only light was from head-mounted lights, my camera flash, and a handheld light I had for fill lighting. We finally got a great photo of Brady emerging from some sawgrass with a good-sized gator, but decided to try one more when he spotted a big one in a deeper canal."

Barr waded into the waist-deep water with the snare, which he snagged around the gator's neck. "It turned out to be much larger than any we had previously caught," Sroka says, "and it

your point of view. Three different photographers could all take the same shot of a lion, but each would be different because each person would bring something of him- or herself to the photo. Each would express a unique point of view about that lion.

Since most photo shoots take place outside of the United States, you may find yourself in cultures far different from your

immediately bolted for the opening of a nearby drainage pipe in the bank of the trail. All three of us grabbed the snare, struggling to prevent the gator from getting into the pipe and escaping. He was using his front legs to pull himself into the pipe—I have never felt such sheer strength."

Only by using the snare's pole as a lever against the gator's shoulder were the three able to pry him out, drag him onto the bank by the tail, and remove the snare. "I finally took a few pictures of Brady sitting on the gator's back, but no one looked very good at that point," Sroka says. The sawgrass picture Sroka had taken earlier that evening was much better, and it appeared in the November 1998 *National Geographic* (page 142).

The best thing about working at the *National Geographic* was the people, Sroka says. "Everyone was really first-rate at what they did. There was a carpentry shop that could build anything—and build it like fine furniture—whether it was a display case or a crate for shipping camera equipment. Even the cafeteria had really fine food. The whole environment made you do your best."

One of the most remarkable people he met at the magazine was Luis Marden, the quintessential world-traveling writer-photographer of the 1950s. "He discovered the remains of the Bounty at Pitcairn Island using very early Aqualung prototypes and the first underwater cameras. He knew Jacques Cousteau and lived in a house built for him by Frank Lloyd Wright. I would be talking to him and he would be interrupted by a phone call, seamlessly converse in some foreign language, then continue our conversation."

If you're interested in becoming a photographer for the *National Geographic*, Sroka recommends that you try to become an assistant to several professional photographers. "Assisting will quickly show you the realities of how much work, and waiting, is involved in creating a really good picture. You'll also see firsthand how someone with experience deals with a variety of situations.

"Find photographers doing the kind of things you're interested in. Work at becoming the best at what you love. Specialize. Build a portfolio of what you're passionate about, work for a local newspaper, just be sure you are sincerely doing what you truly like and doing it well. *National Geographic* magazine and all kinds of publications are always planning and writing new angles on the world—just look at the articles."

Sroka believes that the days of the world-traveling writer/photographer capable of covering any subject are probably long gone, and notes that the magazine no longer maintains a large stable of photographers, because the wealth of freelance talent is so vast. "More and more often I see the bee article illustrated by the expert bee photographer who has been photographing bees for 30 years. The bottom line is, do what you will be really good at, do it well, and with a little effort and timing, they will come to you."

own. It pays to learn how to get along in other countries, to try always to be polite and flexible as you work to get your photos. On each story, the photographer is paired with an illustrations/photo editor at the magazine who will help come up with ideas and make sure they're worthwhile. Then comes the creation of the budget, the details of getting the shoot started—and then it's off to the location. Once you're there, on the scene, the magazine requires you to provide factual details for every shot, such as where the photographs are taken and who's in them. As a result, most photographers take copious notes or carry a small tape recorder with details for every specific frame of every specific roll to be sent back. Many photographers send back unprocessed rolls to the magazine.

At about the halfway point in the assignment, you'll head back to the *Geographic* offices in Washington, D.C. to meet with your editor to check on how the story is going. You and the photo editor produce a "halfway show" of the best photos you've taken to that point, and the two of you discuss how the story is coming with those at the meeting. If things aren't going well, the whole thing could be cancelled, but if everything looks good they'll decide that the story will be finished.

Once you've finished shooting in the field, your job still isn't over; at the *Geographic*, the photographer is involved in offering input during the photographic process from the very beginning right through to the final layout. Once all your photos are in the bag, you'll go back for the final show at headquarters, going through the very best images from the entire assignment. Photographers typically may shoot about 600 to 900 rolls of

36-exposure film, which is an enormous amount to look through to come up with the final dozen or so photos that will end up in the magazine. When the final photos have been chosen, the photographer helps put together the text and pictures. The photographer is also involved in fact checking and caption writing.

If this sounds like a lot of time-consuming work, it is; you can expect your story to appear about one or two years after you've photographed it.

Pitfalls

If you've got a lot of other things going on in your life, you may not have time for the *Geographic*, where a photo assignment can take six to nine months of your life. As a staff photographer, you'll work long hours when you're on a shoot—up before dawn, and working well into the night. To make it as a freelance photographer, it's not enough to have talent—you also have to be able to write and market yourself.

Perks

What could be more exciting for a photographer than to be able to exhibit your work in an internationally acclaimed publication famed for its nature shots? Taking photos for *National Geographic* is also lucrative, and because as a freelancer you'll usually get to keep the rights to your work, you can market your photos elsewhere after they have been published in the magazine.

Get a Jump on the Job

Hone your photographic talents. You can start while you're still in high school by taking any photography classes at school or in your community, and by reading up on techniques. Visit photo exhibits and study books of classical photos, and practice as much as you can. Film is relatively cheap, so practice taking shots at different exposures, different apertures, and different angles.

If your dream is to be a photographer, you may want to investigate the magazine's internships for young photographers. It will also help you if you're good with languages, so spend some time now learning how to communicate with people in other parts of the world. Make sure that you're driven by a love of taking photos—not by travel and meeting other people.

NEWSPAPER BUREAU CHIEF

OVERVIEW

As the bureau chief of a national newspaper or syndicate, you're responsible for assigning and vetting stories from your reporters, correspondents, and from a variety of stringers. You're responsible for getting the news as it happens, and beating everybody else while you're at it. Frequently getting scooped by the competition may result in a one-way ticket back to the small-town trenches.

Bureau chiefs are the crème de la crème of journalists—veteran reporters who have come up through the ranks, covering important local and national stories. Many have worked in the Washington bureau as news reporter, ending up with a bureau appointment by constantly polishing their credentials, winning important awards, and going back to school for advanced degrees.

Yet the life of a bureau chief isn't always settled and predictable. Many don't stay in one city, but may be moved from one city to the next, more desirable city.

Large newspapers and newspaper publishers have bureaus in most major urban areas in the United States and in scores of countries worldwide. Because these bureaus supply content to their newspapers' main office, every minute of every day is their deadline. At heart, the bureau chief is a talented generalist, whose mission is to assign stories as quickly and accurately as possible while also editing all kinds of stories from others—from breaking news to entertainment and sports. The job is fast-paced and varied as bureau chiefs make reporting assignments, plan coverage, train and evaluate the staff, and edit copy. Bureau chiefs also must handle a fair amount of administrative work, including budgeting and intensive recordkeeping.

AT A GLANCE

Salary Range
$80,000 to $120,000+

Education/Experience
A degree in journalism, mass communications, English, or a similar major is required. About 450 colleges offer formal programs in journalism and mass communications.

Personal Attributes
You should be able to tolerate enormous stress and constant deadlines, as well as be flexible, curious, intelligent, honest, and hardworking.

Requirements
In addition to an excellent journalism education and the ability to write quickly and well, you'll need excellent communication and computer skills and the technological know-how to transmit stories from almost anywhere. You'll also need the ability to manage others, since you'll be required to assign stories to all the reporters working in the bureau. Administrative skills are also vital.

Outlook
Keen competition is expected for many jobs on news bureaus in large metropolitan areas, because so many people are attracted by the glamour of this industry. You'll have the best chance if you have a college degree from a top school in journalism, communications, or a related field, as well as relevant work experience.

Most large newspapers maintain bureaus in New York, Washington, D.C., Chicago, Miami, and Los Angeles, as well as international bureaus around the world. Some also maintain smaller bureaus in other large U.S. cities.

John Walcott, Knight Ridder bureau chief

One of Washington, D.C.'s most accomplished national security and foreign affairs journalists, John Walcott started out his career the way most journalists do—he simply wanted to be a reporter. He didn't pay much attention to thoughts of someday becoming an editor or bureau chief—he just wanted to cover the news.

"I don't think anyone gets into the business wanting to be bureau chief or an editor," he says. "I started as a reporter on a tiny newspaper in northern New Jersey that came out twice a week, and after that I went to a daily in northern New Jersey. I covered local towns and school board meetings, police departments."

After three years on the daily, he was sent to Washington, D.C., to work out of their two-person bureau. Two years later, he moved on to work as a reporter for *Newsweek*, where he stayed for nine years, based in D.C. but traveling all over the world. Then it was on to the *Wall Street Journal* D.C. bureau for three more years as a reporter, and then on to become foreign and national editor of *U.S. News and World Report*. "That's when I made the transition from reporter to editor," Walcott says. "I think in any profession, if you're a manager of any sort, you don't want to be in a position of asking other people to do things you haven't done yourself. I'm a great believer in starting at the bottom and working your way up. If you're interested in journalism, go be a reporter or photographer first, whether it's in TV or radio, newspapers, magazines, or online."

Walcott and his staffers report to Knight Ridder readers in cities all over the country about how what happens in Washington and around the world affects the rest of America, not just how it reflects the power struggles in the capital. Walcott says he tries to provide information that can make a difference in the lives of his readers.

As a diplomatic correspondent he covered wars in Lebanon and El Salvador, the Arab-Israeli conflict, and the fall of apartheid in South Africa, reporting from more than 60 countries. During the late 1980s he reported on the Iran-Contra affair and arms control negotiations with the Soviet Union. He directed coverage of the fall of the Berlin Wall, the 1994 "Republican revolution," and the Clinton administration.

His awards include the Freedom of the Press Award from the National Press Club and three Overseas Press Club awards. He is the coauthor, with David C. Martin, of *Best Laid Plans: The Inside Story of America's War Against Terrorism*. He also serves as an adjunct professor in the School of Foreign Service at Georgetown University.

A liberal arts graduate in English from Williams College in Massachusetts, he's a firm believer in the importance of a broad liberal arts education. "Among the ones I think you need to make a point of spending some time on are English, writing, and courses that emphasize reading great writing, political science, history, economics, comparative religion, and art history. And some science and math, particularly statistics, which is not an easy course

Pitfalls

Trying to stay on top of the news for an entire major city or region can be exhausting, and the pressure is nonstop. Very long, irregular hours, night and weekend work, and lots of travel are almost a given, so

for a lot of liberal arts majors. But numbers and metrics are important in reporting. You see a lot of them, people throw a lot of them at you, and being able to tell good from bad is an important skill. The broader the education you have, the better."

The "vocational courses" taught in most journalism schools are less helpful, he believes. "I don't think there's a substitute in a world that is shrinking, for the breadth of a liberal arts education. I think the vocational courses are of less value because the profession is changing so rapidly and profoundly, largely as a result of technology and the economy."

The kind of technology you might learn in journalism school today, he says, may well be out of date in another five years. "The Internet and broadband in particular, and digital recording, are enabling us to tell stories in a way we haven't been able to tell them before, integrating sound and pictures and words. Young people today are going to be the ones who invent that form of storytelling, which would be an exciting reason to get into journalism today. You're getting into a profession that is re-inventing itself. New ideas are more likely to come from someone in school today than someone my age."

In addition to a liberal arts education, Walcott also believes that a foreign language is vital—especially since many bureau chiefs end up working abroad. "If it's Spanish, great. If it's Chinese or Arabic or Japanese, great. But increasingly, two languages are the minimum for working in a global economy, especially if you have some aspiration to work overseas someday. If you do, then take that semester abroad, partly for the language and partly for the experience of living overseas."

If you're dreaming about a journalism career, he also recommends that you work on as many internships as possible. "Journalism is really a craft that is best learned on the job," he explains. "So try to find yourself a place where you'll get good editing, direction, and feedback, and where you'll be required to write early and often."

Having spent more than half his career in the trenches, writing and reporting the news, he does admit that as a bureau chief he gets less time to actually write the news. " I'd rather be out reporting," he admits, "but I still do some reporting and little bit of writing. Nowadays, that's someone else's job and I try not to get in the way."

The only thing he doesn't like about being a bureau chief is the administrative detail, which can be excessive since he's also responsible for administering 10 foreign bureaus. "Baghdad alone keeps me really busy," he says.

"What I like best about being a bureau chief is the same thing I liked about a liberal arts education—I get involved in the broadest range of stories imaginable," he says. "In the course of one day I'll deal with the Mine Safety and Health Administration, the war in Iraq, the rioting among Muslims in Europe, and the federal budget."

you may not spend a lot of time at home with the family.

Perks

If you're a journalist who loves to be in the know, making it all the way to bureau chief is probably a dream come true. As chief, you're privy to all the inside information and you may get your byline on some of the best stories. Nonfiction book deals are also a possibility—and the salary's pretty good, too.

Get a Jump on the Job

If you're pursuing a career in print journalism, you should start by getting some initial experience working at your college paper or in an internship at a newspaper or magazine. Although these positions are usually unpaid, they sometimes provide college credit or tuition. More importantly, they provide hands-on experience and a competitive edge when applying for jobs. As technology is changing, the jobs in news are changing right along with it. The more you can learn about computers, electronic technology, podcasting, and digital photography, the better.

OMBUDSMAN

OVERVIEW

Newspapers have been known as public watchdogs for a long time. But it wasn't long before critics wondered just who was watching the watchdog. That would be the ombudsman, also known as the reader's representative, or public editor. The job originates in Sweden, where the first ombudsman was hired by the government in 1809 to handle citizen complaints. Ombudsmen since have been hired by hospitals, universities, corporations, and other businesses that benefit from public feedback. Although newspapers traditionally invite criticism by printing letters to the editor, that's a far cry from giving readers an advocate who has the ear of management. U.S. newspaper readers got their first ombudsman in 1967 when one was hired for both Louisville newspapers, the *Times* and *Courier-Journal*. Eventually, ombudsmen were working for newspapers in every region of the nation.

As an ombudsman, you'll handle readers' phone calls, e-mails, letters, and any other messages that express compliments, criticism, or questions. Readers may call to point out a factual error or complain about a perceived bias. For instance, some readers may complain the paper is favoring one political party over another or even one high school football team over another. The ombudsman may point out that the reader's favorite party or high school team has received more positive coverage than the reader may have noticed. Or the ombudsman may explain why a story was not as long or as prominently played as a reader may have wanted. Often, the ombudsman

AT A GLANCE

Salary Range
$30,000 to $100,000

Education/Experience
You'll need a college degree, preferably in journalism. Most importantly, you'll need years of newsroom experience to understand the makings of fair and accurate reporting. It also helps to have experience dealing with the public so you can deal effectively and courteously with readers.

Personal Attributes
You need to get along well with people because you'll be dealing with disgruntled readers as well as reporters and editors who may resent the criticism you pass on. You should be patient, even-tempered, and a good listener. You should have a sense of humor because some of the complaints you get will really be off the wall. You'll need a strong sense of ethics and you can't be afraid to speak your mind.

Requirements
You must have a clear and pleasant phone voice to deal with readers. You'll need to write clearly and forcefully because you'll write reports for the news staff that summarize reader complaints. You'll also be expected to write a regular column.

Outlook
Only about 30 U.S. newspapers had ombudsmen when this book was published, so those who hold this job form a small fraternity. Yet not many newsroom employees apply for this job because they're afraid it could throw their careers off track. If you aspire to become an ombudsman, you have a good chance of becoming one.

will agree the reader has a valid point and promise to look into the matter. At the end of each workday, the ombudsman will usually summarize readers' criticisms in a report and deliver them to the newsroom.

No reporters or editors, obviously, enjoy seeing their mistakes or lapses in judgment pointed out. If the newspaper's coverage of a story or issue is especially controversial, the ombudsman usually will address that issue in a regular column.

The *New York Times* was among the newspapers that for a long time resisted hiring an ombudsman. The *Times* was forced to change its position in 2003 when it was revealed that one its reporters, Jayson Blair, had consistently fabricated

Kate Parry, ombudsman

With all the controversies over fairness and accuracy in journalism, one might think that any *Minneapolis Star-Tribune* reader would know that ombudsman Kate Parry is there to handle complaints. But some readers apparently think she should provide other services. "People call me up and say astonishing things, strange things that have nothing to do with journalism," Parry says. "I had an elderly woman call me up and say, 'I've got two big bricks of silver. What should I do with them?' I've had lovers call to ask if I thought, based on their horoscopes, whether they were a good match. People can very funny, purposely or unintentionally. I enjoy that a lot."

It wasn't the chance to be amused that led Parry to become an ombudsman in 2004. "As more and more newspapers have struggled with ethical issues, some in very public scandals, I've been growing more concerned about journalism in general," she says. "This job seemed like a good vantage point for having an impact on the ethical behavior in this newsroom and commenting on the profession to a broader audience. I also enjoy talking to readers. I've been a proponent of civic journalism and directed several major projects in St. Paul that involved a lot of reader contact. I really enjoyed it. The minute I heard the job was open, I knew I wanted it."

Parry has the kind of resume any newspaper would want from an ombudsman. She'd been a reporter, editor, and administrator. When she was just 16, she covered the police department and city hall for a weekly newspaper in suburban Gary, Indiana. She earned a bachelor's degree in journalism and urban studies at Indiana University, then was hired by the *Louisville Courier-Journal* as an intern and correspondent. She became a copy editor at the *Minneapolis Tribune*, which later merged with the *Star*, in 1978. She was a restaurant critic for several years and covered local political and education beats. She joined the rival *St. Paul Pioneer Press* in 1991 as a senior editor, overseeing columnists as well as the coverage of politics, health, education, and the environment. She also directed projects that examined poverty, public safety, and immigration and served as the writing coach and newsroom training director. She's also taught at the University of Minnesota School of Journalism and lectured before several journalism groups and at universities in Tokyo. "I've ended up working near five different ombudsmen," Parry says. "So I've picked up a lot of ideas about the right and wrong way to do the job."

Her vast newspaper experience gives Parry a good handle on a reader's complaint and whether it's legitimate. She can explain an ethical issue or help a reader understand the news process. If a reader complains that the paper ran a photograph of a politician frowning instead

and plagiarized stories. This was a major embarrassment for the *Times*, as well as the rest of U.S. newspapers. The *Times* appointed a committee to investigate newsroom policy and recommend safeguards against another scandal. The committee suggested the hiring of an ombudsman to encourage reader access and monitor complaints. Daniel Okrent became the nation's best-known newspaper ombudsman when he was hired as public editor of the *Times* in October 2003. He reported getting

of smiling, Parry might explain the photo came from a wire service and was the only one available. The complaints aren't nearly as frequent or nasty as she once might've assumed. "Our readers here in Minneapolis are smart, funny, and full of ideas," Parry says. "One of the best surprises in my first few months on this job was that only about a third of them called to complain. And, being Minnesotans, they were quite civil. My ombudsmen colleagues in other cities are pretty entertained by the civility of my readers. I've had readers call to complain and then if we do something about it, they call back to apologize that they complained in the first place. Even when they're really angry, they're very civil and thoughtful for the most part.

"The other two-thirds of the calls and e-mails are compliments or people who just want to have a good conversation about the news or the media. Or they have story ideas. Lots of readers' story ideas are getting in this newspaper, which is terrific. So the job has turned out to have a very creative element I didn't realize would be there. The burden of the job is the volume of response and how hard it is to get away from here to go out in the community and talk to people who might not be calling or e-mailing. I enjoy that and it's hard to pull off. I also find the mob tactics of some of the blogs, as they attempt to clobber journalists into submission, frustrating to observe. I think newspapers should foster well-informed, robust, and public discussion. The blogs that go on the attack seem intent on preventing discussion and just drowning out the other side."

Dealing with reader complaints and writing a daily report could be a job in itself. But an ombudsman also writes a regular column to address an issue that's become a hot button for readers or to explain the news process. After Hurricane Katrina destroyed New Orleans in 2005, Parry in her regular Sunday column addressed readers' anger over the slow federal emergency response and, in some cases, the newspaper's coverage. "I have never seen our readers so angry," she says. "I try to mix approaches. Sometimes I criticize the newspaper for something it's done, sometimes I write about something that went well. I try to do transparency columns that give readers a window on how a newsroom functions. What does a copy editor do? How do reporters work? I've done question-and-answer sessions with top editors. I had a headline contest and challenged readers to write headlines on three stories and the winner got to spend a night on the copy desk. That was stunningly popular. I write about First Amendment issues because I think it's important for readers to understand why those issues are important to them and democracy, not just to journalists. I'm always trying to figure out new approaches to the column. After years of editing, it's a pleasure to write a little again."

more than 45,000 e-mails before the end of 2004. Okrent retired in 2005 and was replaced by Byron Calame.

Ombudsmen don't need sensational scandals to be valuable to their newspapers. They improve the quality of reporting by keeping an eye on the accuracy, fairness, and balance of stories. Readers will have more faith in their newspapers' integrity if they get some access to the decision makers. Ombudsmen help reporters and editors get a better connection with their readers. An ombudsman might even satisfy a complaint that would otherwise turn into a lawsuit. Papers also save their employees' time by channeling reader calls to an ombudsman instead of spreading them around to various departments.

Pitfalls

It can get old spending all day listening to complaints. You might sense animosity from some reporters and editors who don't like seeing their performance questioned. Your workload in the office may prevent you from getting out in the community as much as you'd like. And your bosses may not really want you to be as strong and independent in your criticism of the paper as they told you when you took the job.

Perks

It's a chance to become an important link between your newspaper and community. You'll get the satisfaction of knowing you're helping maintain or improve your newspaper's integrity. You'll handle issues that are stimulating and challenging. You'll give speeches and attend conferences that allow you to travel, sometimes overseas.

Get a Jump on the Job

Become a regular newspaper reader and pay special attention to stories that cover areas or events you know a lot about. Are the stories fair and accurate? Do the writers have a good feel for the subject and people involved? Read the *Columbia Journalism Review* and other publications that examine issues an ombudsman will confront regularly.

POLITICAL COLUMNIST

OVERVIEW

A syndicated political columnist writes a column that appears in more than one newspaper or other publication. There are all types of syndicated columnists in the editorial pages of a newspaper, but the political columnist specializes in covering the political scene.

Sometimes a syndication service approaches a political columnist and asks for permission to sell the columns to other publications. In other cases, it's the columnist who seeks syndication. Getting syndicated can require some intensive effort. You can self-syndicate, which means you shop your column around to different editors and hope they agree to run it, or you can look for a syndication service to do that for you.

If a syndication service agrees to take your column and place it for you, you can expect to pay them about half of what papers pay to run it. The upside is that being represented by a syndication service means that your column probably will appear in more papers than you could find by yourself.

A political columnist must be an astute observer of politics and have a thorough understanding of political systems and the way that politics work. Political columnists are expected to take positions on different issues, and most are known as being conservative, liberal, or moderate.

Political columnists, as is the case with all journalists, are expected to act ethically, presenting information fairly and

AT A GLANCE

Salary Range

Salaries for syndicated political columnists vary tremendously, depending on the number of publications that pay to run the column, the deal the columnist has with the syndicate service, and other factors. Many columnists are employed by a newspaper or magazine, which pays them to write a column. Money from the syndication of the column would be in addition to their base salaries. The average salary for a newspaper political columnist ranges from $23,000 to $47,000, but that includes papers of all sizes in all areas. A well known, syndicated political columnist would earn much more, and would have many opportunities to earn additional money by offering speeches, teaching, serving as a consultant, and so forth.

Education/Experience

You'll need a college degree, preferably in journalism or communications in order to get started. You'll also need a broad background in history, political science, and politics. Some columnists get an undergraduate degree in journalism and then earn a higher degree or degrees in other areas.

Personal Attributes

You'll need to be able to carefully consider an issue and then form a well thought-out discussion of your views relating to that issue. You must be reasonable rather than reactionary, and able to clearly state your views and opinions. You also need to be diligent, task oriented, and able to complete deadlines on time. You should be able to work under stressful conditions and be willing to put in the time necessary to complete a job. You also should be articulate, have good listening skills, and be able to converse with people about a wide variety of topics.

Requirements

Requirements will vary from employer to employer. Most will require newspaper experience, either as

(continues)

AT A GLANCE (continued)

reporter or editor. You'll need to have a wide range of knowledge concerning current events and world issues

Outlook

The outlook for newspapers is not a rosy one, and, as a result, jobs for syndicated political columnists are expected to increase at a rate that is lower than average—only 3 to 9 percent through 2012. Newspapers are struggling with decreasing circulation and advertising profits and increasing expenses. As a result, many are closing, merging, or consolidating.

accurately and avoiding even the appearance of a conflict of interest. Syndicated columnist Maggie Gallagher came under fire in 2002 when, in her column, she repeatedly defended efforts by President Bush to designate $300 million to be used for programs to encourage marriage. The idea was to encourage teens and others to get married first, and have children second. While there was nothing wrong with Gallagher praising the efforts of the president and promoting his proposed program in her syndicated column, many found it disturbing when they learned she also was on the payroll of the U.S. Department of Health and Human Services—a government agency. Her job there, for which she was to be paid more than $20,000, was to help promote Bush's program. Questions were raised as to whether Gallagher should have disclosed her government contract to her readers, and whether using her column to promote the plan was a conflict of interest. You can see how being a political columnist means that you're in the public eye, and subject to close scrutiny.

Pitfalls

Lots of people write columns for newspapers, magazines, and online publications. Very few, however, become nationally known, syndicated political columnists. The competition is keen, and opportunities exist only for those willing to work extremely hard. If you do become a columnist, either syndicated or not, you'll find that you'll be subject to a fair amount of pressure to think of ideas and meet your writing obligations.

Perks

Syndicated political columnists are widely recognized and often are tapped to give speeches, teach, serve as consultants, and perform other jobs that can pay very well. They are also powerful in that they help to shape the opinions of their readers and share their viewpoints with people all over the country—sometimes the world.

Get a Jump on the Job

You can't run before you walk, which means you'll need to work hard at becoming a writer and reporter before you can get to be a syndicated political columnist. Join your school newspaper. Some local papers accept opinion pieces from people in the community. If you know of an issue you feel strongly about and you can present your views accurately, you could offer to write such a piece. Practice writing on a variety of topics, and take all the writing courses that you can fit into your schedule. Also, start reading all the political columnists that run in your local paper, or go online and look them up. Pay attention to how they make their points and how they shape their writing.

Leonard Pitts, Jr., syndicated political columnist

Leonard Pitts, Jr. is a Washington, D.C.-based columnist for the *Miami Herald*. His twice-weekly column, which is syndicated by Tribune Media Services, appears not only in the *Herald*, but in more than 200 other papers across the country.

Interestingly, Pitts' writing career started with music reviews. While he was still in college, Pitts wrote freelance reviews for *SOUL*, a national black entertainment tabloid. He later became the editor of *SOUL*, and in 1991 he was hired as the pop music critic for the *Miami Herald*. While he says he has always loved music, his primary goal since he was five years old was to be a writer. Over time, his interests shifted toward politics and social issues. Pitts also is the author of several books, and has written and produced radio documentaries.

What he likes most about being a syndicated political columnist is the opportunity it gives him to have his voice heard concerning issues he feels strongly about. "I appreciate the ability to have a voice in the national debate, especially when the news is frustrating or infuriating to me," Pitts says. "There are days when I feel like, if I wasn't able to vent in the newspaper, my head would pop off my neck like a balloon."

He also enjoys the variety that his job offers. "There's no such thing as a typical day, that's for sure. A little over a week ago, I was sitting in my office at Ohio University preparing to teach classes. The next day, much to my surprise, I was on the road in an RV to cover the aftermath of Hurricane Katrina," Pitts says.

Pitts acknowledged that coming up with ideas on which to base two columns a week can be difficult, and sometimes frustrating. However, he's found that a new idea is never too far away. "I run out of ideas just about every week," Pitts says. "But you learn to be patient. Something always comes."

Pitts can write about anything he wants, as long as he thinks his readers will find it interesting. This gives him great freedom to explore a variety of ideas, situations, and circumstances, and ensures that he'll never get bored.

"There is little structure and less predictability to my days," he says. "The only constant is the need to produce a column twice a week. After that, anything goes."

RADIO DISC JOCKEY

OVERVIEW

Radio disc jockeys select and place music on the radio. They also introduce the music and talk about various topics in order to inform and entertain listeners. Some radio stations put two DJs on the air at the same time so that they can interact with one another. Some DJs encourage listeners to call in and participate in the show. There is a great deal of variation in radio formatting, and disc jockeys are expected to operate within the formatting the station has in place.

Radio DJs work in studios, which are small, soundproof rooms from which a show is broadcast. They also sometimes use portable sound studios contained in vans or trucks to broadcast from various locations. Typically, that is done when an advertiser wants to draw attention to a new shop, special sale, or other event. The live broadcast is intended to attract people to the location.

Some disc jockeys are responsible for delivering commercials. At some small stations, the DJ may even be required to write the advertising copy, although most radio stations have advertising staff to do that. The job varies tremendously, depending on location and size of the station.

Radio disc jockeys typically work four-hour shifts, five or six days a week. It's very important that a DJ is able to make his or her listeners feel comfortable and entertained. That means that the disc jockey should sound sincere and interesting, with a pleasant voice and good timing.

AT A GLANCE

Salary Range

The average earnings for radio disc jockeys range between $7.15 and $15.10 per hour, according to the U.S. Bureau of Labor Statistics. Those in the lowest 10 percent of the salary bracket earn less than $6.20, while the highest-paid earned more than $25 an hour. Disc jockeys at large radio stations in cities can expect to earn much more than those at small stations in small towns or rural areas.

Education/Experience

There are no set educational requirements to be a disc jockey, but taking some classes at a technical school or a college is beneficial. Some schools offer a broadcast journalism course. Other useful classes may include English, drama, and speech.

Personal Attributes

You need to be comfortable in front of a microphone and able to connect with your listeners. You must have a pleasant, well-controlled voice, and be able to maintain a dialogue. Being on the air can be stressful, so you need to be able to remain calm and cool if things don't go exactly as planned. You should have a good command of language, be interested in current events, and be able to establish relationships with other people. In short, you need to be interesting and well informed in order to keep listeners interested in you.

Requirements

Disc jockeys are subject to the rules of the Federal Communications Commission, an agency that regulates interstate and international communications, including those by radio, television, satellite, cable, and wire. Individual radio stations may have additional requirements.

Outlook

Sadly, the outlook for radio disc jockeys is not very good. The number of DJ jobs actually is expected to decrease through 2012, partially due to very limited

(continues)

AT A GLANCE *(continued)*

growth in the number of radio stations. Radio stations are being centralized, which reduces the number of workers needed. There's also a growing trend for stations to operate without disc jockeys, relying on satellite feeds or pre-taped broadcasts.

Employers will look for these qualities when you apply for jobs. You'll be asked to do a taped audition, which employers will scrutinize for style, how well you can ad lib, how your voice sounds, and other considerations.

Pitfalls

Getting a job as a radio disc jockey is extremely competitive, and you may have

Rick Stuart, radio disc jockey

Rick Stuart grew up listening to the radio. He liked the music, but also liked listening to the disc jockeys. His first experience behind the microphone came when he was a broadcasting major and worked at KUSF at the University of San Francisco.

He taught himself how to be a DJ by modeling his show after one he liked on the local radio station.

"At first, I would tape the local top 40 station and go by the songs they played. Then I would write down word for word what the DJ says, and would try to repeat his show on the college station. I'd talk over the intros of the songs the same way he did and mix the music the same way. Pretty much, I'd say exactly what he had said. I did the commercials the same way, the PSAs [public service announcements], everything."

As he became more experienced, however, Stuart found his own style, which has become very popular in the San Francisco area, where he's known as Big Rick Stuart. He has worked at about half a dozen radio stations in and around San Francisco, thoroughly enjoying even his first full-time job, which was the midnight to 6 a.m. shift.

"I love the fun of each day at work being different," Stuart says. "Unlike acting in a play, in radio, every time you talk it's something different. And, unlike TV or movies, when you do a radio show, it's over as soon as you're done talking. It's a challenge to entertain that way, without a script."

The hardest part of being a DJ for Stuart is being constantly upbeat for his audience.

"You can't come to work and just slack off if you're tired or in a bad mood," he says. "You can't show up late or go home early. You have to kind of build a wall between anything bad that may have happened in your day and the time you're on the air. When you're in the studio and turn on the mike, people are tuning in to have you pick them up and play their favorite music. You always have to remember that."

Stuart advises anyone interested in becoming a radio disc jockey to get some voice training, if possible.

"That will help you to use your voice and develop a stage presence," he says. "Even though you're on the radio, part of your job is acting."

And, he says, be on the lookout for internships, especially once you get to the college level. It's also a good idea to listen to a lot of radio, and take notice of what the DJs have in common, despite the type of music they play.

to be prepared to take what comes along, regardless of whether or not it's what you really would like. Many stations are on the air 24 hours a day, meaning that your first job could very well be the midnight to 6 a.m. shift. And, even if you're feeling crummy or you have a big problem you're trying to deal with, you'd better show up for work sounding in control and happy to be there. That goes for bad weather, too. If it snows overnight, it's going to be especially important for the DJ to be on the air to advise listeners of school closings, traffic problems, and so forth.

Perks

Being a disc jockey is fun, and it gives you a level of celebrity. Radio disc jockeys often are asked to attend special events, or to host or serve as master of ceremony at parties, auctions, and fund-raisers. People who listen to a disc jockey over a period of time come to feel that they know the DJ, and generally respond positively.

Get a Jump on the Job

If your school has a radio station, be sure to volunteer. Anything you can do to get comfortable behind a microphone will be useful, so you might also consider volunteering to provide DJ services at a school or community dance or announcing at a sporting event. Read everything you can about being a disc jockey, and practice speaking and maintaining a running dialogue. Get involved in school and/or community theater and get some acting experience. Visit a radio station and ask if you can talk to a disc jockey. Listen to all the radio that you can, including as many different formats as you can find.

RADIO REPORTER

OVERVIEW

Radio reporters have the same goal as any other reporters—to gather information and get it first. And they use the same methods—research, interviews, and hustle. But their tools are different. So are their advantages and disadvantages. Despite the dramatic new technology in all areas of journalism, radio still offers the most instantaneous news. A reporter using a satellite phone can send a live radio report from the world's remotest places. Radio news may be updated with fresh reports several times within the hour, while TV usually has to keep showing the same footage. Newspapers can't publish news until the next morning and have to settle for posting reports on their Web sites. And newspapers and TV stations don't get into our car during rush hour, or "drive time," when radio rules.

Because radio reporters don't have pictures, they must provide high-quality information, interviews, and sound. For news coverage of a dramatic event such as a fire, a TV picture truly is worth a thousand words. A radio reporter must describe the fire in such detail that the listener can almost smell the smoke. There might be interviews with firefighters, victims, and witnesses, and sounds of panicky voices and breaking glass. A radio report also must get quickly to the point and be clearly understood. Unlike a newspaper story, it can't go into great detail or be reread.

AT A GLANCE

Salary Range

$12,000 to $60,000

Education/Experience

Although you can find some old-school radio reporters without college degrees, don't count on having a successful career without one. Many universities offer courses in radio journalism and most have their own stations to give students experience. A lot of reporters get started at small stations, then climb the ladder.

Personal Attributes

You must react quickly to breaking news and handle deadline pressure. You should be a people person because the best reporters make the people they interview feel at ease and important. And you should have a competitive fire because you'll be trying to break the story before rival television, newspaper, and radio reporters.

Requirements

You don't need a classic broadcast voice but you do need a voice that's clear and smooth. You need good interviewing skills and the ability to describe news events without the benefit of pictures. You must be able to use the technology for editing your recordings. And you'll be expected to be familiar with a wide variety of subjects.

Outlook

Radio has survived the onslaught of broadcasting competition and will need reporters for many years to come. People breaking in will have to be patient, though, because jobs for beginners, especially in small markets, offer very low pay.

A radio reporter must pay special attention to the quality of sound and information that he or she records. If you carefully watch television news, especially sports, you'll notice that many interviews are so poor that they'd be useless without the pictures. But a radio interview better have meat on its bones. Getting people to agree to interviews is a key part of any reporter's job. But many people would rather appear on television than radio because it's more glamorous to be on camera. Yet good radio reporters get interviews from those people, too, as well as scoops from sources who'd rather be interviewed on radio because they don't want to be identified. They may be witnesses to a crime, playing

Dan Verbeck, radio reporter

When Dan Verbeck is on the air in Kansas City, his passion for breaking news is matched only by his passion for local history. "I think it's important to know your community, and what else does a community have besides history?" he asks. "It makes for a better story if you can drop something historic in." So when a midtown Kansas City police station was being renovated, Verbeck informed KMBZ listeners that the building marked the site where Jesse James's wife died. Or he'll tell them that Carrie Nation, the famous anti-alcohol crusader, was buried in 1911 in nearby Belton, Missouri, and that her first husband, a doctor who hailed from that town, was an alcoholic.

Verbeck became intrigued in 2005 when a police officer told him that an urn holding a woman's ashes had been on a property room shelf for 20 years. Verbeck learned that the woman, Bernice Hickmon, died in 1983, and relatives left her ashes in a home they sold. The new owner turned the ashes over to the police two years later but nobody claimed them. Verbeck suggested the ashes deserved a proper resting place. He cooperated with police, a funeral home and a cemetery to arrange a funeral that was complete with a police chaplain, police honor guard, and floral arrangement.

Verbeck was leaning toward a newspaper career before he joined the Army in 1965. The Army sent him to a broadcasting school in Indianapolis, where instructors tried to rid him of his Chicago accent. Verbeck kept the accent but was drawn to radio and found a job at a small station in Atchison, Kansas. "I liked the concept of it—the speed of getting news on the air," he says. "I replaced a guy who had a heart attack in the middle of a newscast. Not a lot of people were listening and they had 20 minutes of dead air—literally—until somebody called and says, 'You're not on the air.' My predecessor was sitting at his desk, keeled over." Verbeck's next stop was St. Joseph, Missouri, where he directed a small news staff. Between radio jobs, he tended bar at a St. Joseph country club. "I met some members of the city council there," Verbeck recalls. "At my first city council meeting as a reporter, I told one councilman, 'You don't know me, but I know you as a double gin and tonic.' He looked at me like I was insane."

Verbeck worked his way up to KMBZ in Kansas City, where he's been a featured reporter on the morning news show from 5 to 9. Twice a week he arrives at work at 12:30 a.m. and prepares "Verbeck's Kansas City," a segment that allows him to showcase his knowledge of the area and its history. The rest of the week, he starts at 2:30 a.m. by checking his police scanner. "I'm talking to people by 3:15 or 3:30," he says. "Cops, dispatchers, people working in all-night restaurants, people who work in street departments. When I have something and it's in the newspaper two days later, I feel pretty good. I look forward to going to work almost every day. The unknown is waiting out there and I want to make it known. I think everybody in this business

hooky from work or school, or have legal problems of their own.

Radio reporters consider themselves the foot soldiers of broadcasting. They announce their reports with a strong, rapid delivery that gives the news a special sense of urgency. Radio reporters often add a highly personal touch. By asking the right questions and putting a subject at ease, a skillful reporter can turn an interview into a warm personal conversation. Radio reporters must think on their feet and ask

has to go out every day with a sense of curiosity, an open mind, and a good pair of boots in the front seat of your car. You never know what you're going to run into. Sometimes you have to go where the roads are not accessible."

Verbeck's sense of adventure led him into the arms of Hurricane Katrina, which destroyed New Orleans in August 2005. KMBZ's parent company, Entercom, asked him to help its New Orleans station, WWL, with hurricane coverage. That was before anyone realized how much devastation would result. Verbeck's aggressive reporting and ability to work without much sleep came in handy when broken levees flooded most of the city. WWL became the major news source for those who were stranded because they didn't get out before the flooding. Verbeck, working on the streets and in the studio, was part of a skeleton crew who worked tirelessly for four days. He'd never witnessed so much death and misery. "I thought I'd seen it all," he says. "But that was the zenith. And I wasn't prepared for it in my head."

The hurricane took Verbeck back to an era in which listeners leaned on radio as their main source for major news events, presidential speeches, and weather warnings. When he came home, Verbeck returned to a world in which radio stations fight tooth and nail against other stations and other media. "People listen to radio in the morning and watch TV at night," he says. "TV wants pictures but radio will always be a theater of the mind, where you have to take them there. Sometimes you do it with a simple declarative sentence. Sometimes on deadline, you just ad-lib and describe what you're smelling and seeing. You also have to measure your cadence to fit the story. What still annoys me is to hear a reporter or anchor relate a soul-tearing story with the same kind of voice you'd use to report a business story. I don't want to hear a reporter blubbering, but if your voice betrays a little of what's going on, it's being human. And you can't act—it's got to come naturally. If you try to phony it up, you betray yourself and betray your profession."

Verbeck estimates he's covered 10,000 homicides but tries not to become hardened to anyone's misfortune or grief. "Every reporter has his own style," he says. "Some stick a microphone in somebody's face and say, 'How do you feel now that your family just died?' It never works for me. I have to talk to people first. That's when people reveal things. You have to be engaging enough that people want to trust you. People tell me things and it's understood they'll never be quoted. One guy called me for 10 years and he'd say, 'Tell Dan that Mister X is on the phone.' He knew about a lot of things. This job is about people—the good people, the scoundrels, the heroic people. Telling their stories sometimes is more important than the events going on around them."

the right follow-up questions so they tie up a story's loose ends. And they should keep the questions brief.

Most radio reporters have college degrees and cut their teeth at university stations. Many got their first jobs in small markets and developed the skills and resumes that impressed stations in bigger markets. Most radio reporters are full-time employees of local stations or networks. But there also are many freelancers, who may specialize in sports or foreign coverage and work for several outlets. While some radio reporters may have golden throats, a great voice isn't necessary. It's more important to have a strong, clear, and authoritative voice. It's even more important to have the talent and drive to rush to a news scene and be as prepared and knowledgeable as possible.

Pitfalls

Radio reporters often get fired when a station hires a fresh news director who wants to shake things up. They seldom get as much recognition as their more visible rivals on television. Those who work during morning rush hour are up before the crack of dawn. A technical problem, such as dead batteries in a recorder or a nearby magnetic field that wipes out a tape, can make the job stressful. Salaries are relatively low, especially for those starting out in small markets.

Perks

Most radio reporters look forward to work every day. They love the immediacy of radio coverage and competition with other reporters. You'll meet interesting people from every walk of life, from a homeless person to the President of the United States. You'll usually be roving around your community and won't be tied down to a desk.

Get a Jump on the Job

If your school has a radio station, volunteer for any opening. Listen to local and national radio news and note each reporter's information and delivery. Record your own voice while you read a news story, then play it back. Do you like what you hear? Practice to make your voice clearer, smoother, and more authoritative.

SPORTS COLUMNIST

OVERVIEW

A sports columnist reports and offers commentary on items and events relating to sports. He or she might tell the story of an athlete who has overcome tremendous obstacles, or write about and comment on fan behavior at a particular sporting event. A columnist might offer an opinion on a surprising outcome of a game or match, or write about someone in the sports community who needs help.

While sportswriters report the outcomes of games and matches, sports columnists have the opportunity to delve into why those outcomes came to be, and to give the reader glimpses of the athletes and the behind-the-scenes action. It's also expected that sports columnists will express their opinions concerning actions and outcomes of athletes, games, and sports programs in general.

While at large papers a sports columnist may do nothing but write a certain number of columns a week, smaller and mid-sized papers often rely on sports columnists to perform other duties, as well. A columnist may schedule shifts, help to edit copy, and plan coverage in addition to writing columns.

Often, a sports columnist also serves as a sports writer. He or she will cover a sporting event and also write a column about some aspect of the event. For example, during the course of covering a college basketball game, a sports columnist finds out that the team's best player is extremely stressed out because he learned just before

AT A GLANCE

Salary Range

A sports columnist for a mid-sized newspaper can expect to earn between $32,000 and $53,000 a year, depending on how long he or she has worked there, job performance, the paper's location, and other factors. Columnists for large, city papers and high-profile magazines will earn considerably more, while columnists for small papers or other publications will earn less.

Education/Experience

Some sports writers and columnists enter the field from other backgrounds, but you'll probably need a bachelor's degree in journalism or mass communications, preferably with a concentration in sports writing.

Personal Attributes

Sports columnists should be thorough in conducting research and interviews. You must have the concentration skills to keep your mind on what the person you're talking to is telling you. It's very important to listen well, and not have a preconceived idea of what your interviewee is going to say. You must have good writing skills, the ability to communicate your thoughts effectively, and an ability to talk comfortably with people you don't know.

Requirements

Requirements will vary, depending on where you work. You'll probably be required to have a valid driver's license and an accessible vehicle. You'll need press credentials to allow you access into sporting events and other gatherings.

Outlook

The outlook for newspapers is not great, and, as a result, jobs for sports columnists are expected to increase at a rate that is lower than average— only 3 to 9 percent through 2012. Newspapers are struggling with decreasing circulation and

(continues)

AT A GLANCE *(continued)*

advertising profits and increasing expenses. As a result, many are closing, merging, or consolidating. However, jobs may be found on sports-related Web sites, magazines, and other publications.

the game started that his younger brother had been involved in a serious car accident back in his hometown. The coach gave the player the option of not playing and going home immediately, but, after weighing the situation carefully, the player decided to stay because he knew it would be better for the team, and at that point, there was nothing that he could do for his brother.

The sports columnist would write a regular game story, recounting who won, who lost, what the score was, and high points of the game. In that story, he or she might mention that the star player was in the game, despite serious personal concerns. In a column that appears in the paper the following day or a couple of days later, however, the sports columnist could go into detail about the incident. He or she could talk to the player and then write about what the player was feeling during the game, how he held it together on the court, and provide some information about the player's brother.

It requires a high level of objectivity to be able to write a game story exactly the way it happened and keep it separated from a column, in which your own thoughts and opinions can be voiced. Sports columnists must be committed to maintaining high ethical standards as well as a high level of professionalism.

Pitfalls

Sportswriting has long been a popular career, which means it's also a competitive one. Newspapers and other publications (except for the major ones) don't tend to be the highest-paying jobs around. Being a sports columnist can involve significant travel if you're assigned to cover a team or a particular athlete. And, you can't expect to be working banker's hours because sports occur at all times, including nights and weekends.

Perks

If you enjoy watching, analyzing, talking about, and writing about sports, you'll probably love being a sports columnist. When you're a columnist, as opposed to a straight sports reporter, you're free to offer your opinion on the topics you write about, something that many writers consider to be a bonus. You're bound to meet some interesting people, and sports writers and columnists tend to enjoy a nice level of camaraderie amongst themselves.

Get a Jump on the Job

Read all the sports columnists that you can find in magazines, newspapers, and on line. Listen to sports commentators on ESPN or other sports networks and on radio shows. This will start to give you an idea of different writing styles, the types of topics sports columnists tackle, and how a column is organized and presented. Jot down your thoughts about what you read—if you like it or not, and why, and so forth. Practice interviewing people—even your friends—to develop skills. Write for your school newspaper and start an online sports discussion group with your friends.

Rich Scarcella, sports columnist

Rich Scarcella, a sports columnist who covers the Penn State Nittany Lions football team for a mid-sized Pennsylvania newspaper, knew from the time he was 13 years old that he wanted to cover sports and write for a newspaper.

"I feel like I was lucky," Scarcella says. "By the time I was in eighth grade, I knew what I wanted to do."

Knowing what he wanted to do provided Scarcella with direction. He joined his high school newspaper and yearbook staffs. Once he got to college at Pennsylvania State University, he joined the college's newspaper, the *Daily Collegian*, and covered men's volleyball, soccer, men's and women's gymnastics, and football.

"All of those experiences helped to prepare me for my career," he says. "I realize that most people don't know what they want to do as early in life as I did, but, I think if you have an idea, you should start to gain experience as it becomes available to you."

Between his junior and senior years of college, Scarcella landed an internship with the sports department of his hometown paper. He was hired as a sportswriter shortly after graduating from Penn State and has been working as a writer and columnist ever since, covering a wide variety of sports.

"There's been a lot of diversity in my coverage," he says. "I've covered school sports, college sports, big-time major league sports, and minor league sports."

Scarcella loves writing, especially columns.

"I love my work," he says. "What I like most about being a columnist is the freedom to express my opinion and to tell the story behind the story. There's always a lot more to a game than you read about in the game story."

He also enjoys the moderate amount of traveling that comes with his job, and how he's been able to balance his work with his family life.

One thing Scarcella struggles with is the level of celebrity that comes with being a sports columnist. Penn State football is huge in Pennsylvania, and every fan has his or her own set of opinions. If Scarcella expresses an opinion in a column that doesn't agree with a diehard fan, he's sure to hear about it.

"It's all that some people want to talk about," Scarcella says. "Even after all these years, I'm still surprised at how serious some people are about sports. There's one guy who must spend all his time on the Internet, looking up everything that's being written about Penn State football so that he can send it to me. I'm amazed that people devote their whole lives to sports."

Scarcella encourages anyone interested in becoming a sportswriter or sports columnist to do three things: dream, persevere, and read.

"If you want to be a writer, you've got to know how to read," he says. "Read a book. Read the *New York Times* and *Washington Post*. Read *Time* and *Newsweek*. Read everything, and pay attention to what you're reading. You'll be surprised at how much you'll learn."

And, he says, keep your goals in front of you and don't hesitate to pursue them.

"Most importantly, don't be afraid to go after your dream," Scarcella says.

TV NEWS ANCHOR

OVERVIEW

It may look like just buckets of fun, sitting there on the couch as Meredith, Matt, and Al trade jokes on the *Today Show*—but that apparently effortless joshing and casual approach to the news hides years of incredible hard work and dedication. It might look like a lot of fun to be a "news reader," but there's a lot more that's involved behind the scenes.

TV news anchors analyze, interpret, and broadcast news, present news stories, and introduce videotaped news or live transmissions from on-the-scene reporters. At the same time, they may conduct live TV interviews and ask questions on air of a TV reporter at the scene. All the while, the news producer is shouting directions in their ears via earphones.

The work of news anchors is usually hectic, and they're under great pressure to meet deadlines. Broadcasts sometimes must be produced with little or no time for preparation, so the ability to be flexible and handle pressure while on live TV is essential.

If you're just starting out as an anchor, you'll probably land an early-morning or weekend slot, which means you'd need to come to work several hours before you had to be on the air to prepare for your show. For example, a news anchor slated to appear during the live news shows from 5 a.m. to 7 a.m. would typically jump out of bed at 3 a.m. to get to the station by 3:45 a.m. Once at work, you'd look over the scripts for that day's shows. By 4:30

AT A GLANCE

Salary Range

Salaries for anchors vary tremendously depending on the size of the station, the market, and the area of the country, ranging from about $15,000 in the smallest markets to several million in the largest. Star anchors (the highest paid at their stations) draw big money—more than $1 million—which can be about $2 or $3 million in New York or Los Angeles. Even the median is many times higher in the 25 largest markets (about $233,000) than in the 60 smallest ($41,000).

Education/Experience

A degree in broadcast journalism or similar major is required; some type of broadcasting experience is helpful. About 450 colleges offer formal programs in journalism and mass communications, including TV broadcasting, and some community colleges offer two-year programs in broadcasting. Broadcast trade schools offer courses that last six months to a year and teach TV announcing, writing, and production. Practical experience is the most important part of an anchor's broadcast training. Upon college graduation many students have already gained a lot of practical experience through part-time or summer jobs or through internships with news organizations. Most broadcast news organizations offer reporting and editing internships. Work on high school and college broadcasting stations also provides practical training.

Personal Attributes

Neat, well groomed appearance; ability to work long, hard hours; ability to meet deadlines; attention to detail; honesty and credibility.

Requirements

An excellent speaking voice, grace under pressure, the ability to feel relaxed on camera, and a reasonably attractive appearance. Many stations require a degree in journalism or communications, plus broadcast experience.

(continues)

AT A GLANCE *(continued)*

Outlook

Employment in broadcasting is expected to increase almost 9 percent through 2012. Factors contributing to the relatively slow rate of growth include industry consolidation, introduction of new technologies, and competition from other media outlets. Extraordinarily keen competition is expected for many TV news anchor jobs in all markets, because so many people are attracted by the glamour of this industry. You'll have the best chance if you have a college degree in broadcast journalism, communications, or a related field, as well as relevant work experience. Typically, news anchors begin in entry-level positions at smaller TV stations and slowly move up the ladder to larger stations in different areas. The number of job openings in the broadcasting industries is sensitive to economic ups and downs, because these industries depend on advertising revenue.

---

a.m., you'll get to the make up room and at 4:45 a.m. you'd begin the first of your newscasts with a live "teaser" that appears before the actual broadcast begins at 5 a.m. sharp. After your morning broadcasts, you might go out on assignment. For example, a fire breaks out after 7 a.m. You'd be out there covering that from 7 a.m. to 9 a.m. You also might do special projects—investigative, consumer, or health reports with a local angle. Maybe you'd go on-site to interview some local emergency room doctors about how they'd handle an outbreak of bird flu, or perhaps you'd do a special show about drug abuse at a local high school.

Although anchors on morning shows often must come in extremely early in the morning, during an emergency they may need to alter their hours to follow late-breaking developments. Their work demands long hours, irregular schedules, and some travel to cover major stories. Because many stations and networks are on the air 24 hours a day, anchors can expect to work unusual hours, especially early in their careers.

Most anchors start at small broadcast stations as general assignment reporters or stringers; large stations hire few recent graduates. As a rule, stations require new reporters to have several years of experience. After working as a news writer or on-air news reporter, the individual moves to larger stations in more urban markets. As reporters gain more on-air experience, they wait for a slot to open for a fill-in anchor, a weekend or very late night or very early morning anchor. If the person does well, improves ratings, and seems to be popular with the public, the new anchor may be moved into a more visible position doing the daily news or—even better—the evening news.

However, many broadcast anchors begin the upward climb by moving from one station to a slightly larger station in another market, slowly moving up to more responsible positions in bigger cities. It is unusual for someone to spend an entire broadcasting career at one station. Broadcast employees may be eligible to join a union; the principal unions representing employees in broadcasting are the National Association of Broadcast Employees and Technicians (NABET), the International Alliance of Theatrical Stage Employees (IATSE), and the American Federation of Television and Radio Artists (AFTRA).

Pitfalls

TV news anchors work under a great deal of pressure in order to meet deadlines. As a result, they are likely to experience varied or erratic work schedules, often working on early morning or late evening news programs. Broadcast journalism—especially on-air positions—can be extraordinarily stressful, as you must cope not just with how you look but your ratings as well. No matter how attractive you are or how well you think you do your job, your job is probably not secure. If the ratings slide with you as an anchor or management thinks the TV audience would prefer someone younger-thinner-blonder than you, you may be out of a job. In the past, the stability of anchor jobs has been especially uncertain for women, whose age and appearance may be under particular

Jorge Quintana, WFMZ-TV anchor

Growing up in Nicaragua, Jorge Quintana had always been fascinated by TV and wondered what went on behind the scenes. Once he moved to the United States at age 11 and he became aware of the struggles his family experienced as first-generation immigrants, he became interested in helping the Hispanic community.

"When I was in college, I majored in communications with an emphasis in broadcasting," he says, "not knowing what I really wanted to do in TV." At the University of Nevada at Las Vegas, he was required to complete an internship; he landed a spot with a local station KTNV in Las Vegas. "And then the journalism bug bit me," he says. "I've been fascinated with broadcast journalism since then."

After he graduated, he started working behind the scenes and reporting in English; his first job was as a reporter covering immigration and border-related issues for KSWT, the CBS-affiliate in Yuma, Arizona. "I was the only reporter in the newsroom who spoke Spanish, and so they always sent me across the border into Mexico for stories. That's how I discovered that Spanish-speaking issues were so important. I knew that's what I wanted to do, to inform Spanish-speaking people and immigrants."

From there he became the investigative-consumer reporter and anchor for KLUZ, the Univision affiliate in Albuquerque, New Mexico—and then it was on to WFMZ in Allentown, Pennsylvania, to be the 11 p.m. anchor on the only Spanish-language newscast in the Philadelphia region, *Edición en Español*, which includes southern Pennsylvania, New Jersey, and northern Delaware. He works from 2:30 p.m. to midnight, with weekends off—the dream schedule for an anchor.

Jorge's career has given him the opportunity to report on a number of stories that have made national and international headlines, and his work has aired on Univision's national news magazine *Primer Impacto*. But the stories that really interest him are the ones that he spends weeks working on for the benefit of the Hispanic community.

(continues)

scrutiny by the "front office"—whether or not this is completely legal.

Perks

Few news positions are so exciting or glamorous—and well paid—as an anchor slot. Becoming an anchor is usually the culmination of many years of hard work and is a highly visible and rewarding position.

Get a Jump on the Job

If you're pursuing a career in broadcasting, you should try to get some experience working at college radio and TV stations or through internships at professional stations. This way, you'll end up with a tape of your reporting or anchoring that you can use to look for a job later on. Although these positions are usually unpaid, they

---

(continued)

"The best thing about the job is that in a way, you are a little expert in a lot of different fields," he says. "You interview physicians, politicians, teachers, scientists, and you learn so much. And what you learn is what you use to inform the viewers. So every day you learn something new—you're like a little encyclopedia. I think that's what I enjoy—being able to use that information to hopefully change and help someone's life."

The job of a broadcast anchor starts out small, he explains, when you land a job with a small city and move on to larger metropolitan areas. "That's our corporate ladder," he says. "At first, when you start, you're so full of energy, you want to discover every single corner. This is my fifth state! Then it comes to a point you don't want to move any more, you want to settle down and have your kids."

The job of an anchor—like many jobs in broadcast journalism—is inherently precarious, however. "Tomorrow, we might get a new news director, and he might say: 'I don't like my 11 o'clock anchor'—and you're out of a job."

While he loves journalism, being a TV anchor also means he's a bit of a local celebrity. "You're a journalist, you just want to inform people," he says, "but you kind of become a celebrity. You always have to watch what you're doing. I wish people would recognize me more for my work. I wish they would tell me: 'That story you did, I called that number and it did help me.' Instead, they say: 'What do you think if you do your hair this way?' Sometimes I don't shave and I'm at the grocery store and people point that out."

Nevertheless, he loves what he's doing, and he'd encourage anyone else with a journalism dream to try. "It's a very, very competitive field and could be very discouraging," he cautions. "But don't give up. You need to have thick skin. Someone might like the way you speak, might not like the way you speak. You have to take everyone's comments and just smile, even if they're negative. Use it so you can grow."

Like many jobs, the hardest part is at the beginning. "Right now I have a friend who just graduated from college in the L.A. area, and he's very disappointed because he can't get a job. I keep telling him: 'If it's what you want to do, don't give up.'"

sometimes provide college credit or tuition. More importantly, they provide hands-on experience and a competitive edge when applying for jobs. In this highly competitive industry, broadcasters are less willing to provide on-the-job training and instead seek candidates who can perform the job immediately.

Once you graduate from college, you'll have to start out at a small station and work your way up—a rough prospect that may take years. The beauty of starting out at a small station is that you can make mistakes while you're still unknown.

TV NEWS ASSIGNMENT DESK EDITOR

OVERVIEW

Television assignment desk editors are vitally important to a TV newsroom. Assignment desk editors manage news crews, decide who is going where, monitor scanners, and process tips and leads concerning breaking news. They soothe disgruntled reporters, make sure all stories are properly covered, and, generally, manage information.

Often, however, out of sight is out of mind. While on-air personalities get the attention, assignment desk editors often crawl out of the door at night unnoticed. To a person who thrives on pressure and runs on adrenaline, however, there's nothing like this job.

TV assignment desk editors have been described as the air traffic controllers of the television newsroom, directing traffic and heading off disasters. They must always be aware of what is going on, continually in the know and on top of stories, and certain that reporters have met their obligations. When something goes wrong, it's practically a sure bet that it's the assignment editor who will be blamed.

An editor who gets a call about a major fire across town and sends out a crew to cover it, only to have them find out the fire was minor and was completely out by the time the crew arrived, is sure to be in the hot seat. If the editor hadn't sent out the crew, however, and it turned out there was a major fire across town, the consequences would be dire. In short, TV assignment editors often need to have thick skin.

AT A GLANCE

Salary Range

Salaries for television assignment desk editors vary depending on the TV market and location. Average salaries, however, ranged from a low of $27,000 to a high of $55,300. However, some TV assignment desk editors earned significantly more, while others earned less.

Education/Experience

While it used to be that TV desk editors could learn on the job, it's almost certain these days that you'll need a college degree in journalism or communications.

Personal Attributes

There's a lot of pressure to working as a TV assignment desk editor, so you've got to be able to think on your feet and make decisions quickly. You need to have a nose for news, and be able to decide quickly which stories are the most important and should lead the broadcast. You should be able to multitask, as in being able to talk on the phone to someone calling with breaking news while getting together a crew to go cover the story. You also need to be detail oriented.

Requirements

Requirements, such as submitting to drug tests or vehicle use regulations, will vary from employer to employer. You probably will need to have some experience as a TV news reporter before moving to the editor's desk.

Outlook

Positions for television assignment desk editors are expected to increase by between 10 and 20 percent through 2012. This is considered average growth.

While many people who aspire to work in TV news want to be in front of the camera, some thrive on the pressures of working the desk. There are indications that, as TV stations find themselves having an increasing number of problems finding good desk people, salaries for those jobs will increase.

Many TV assignment desk editors say that the longer you do the job, the easier it becomes, because you learn to trust your instincts, make better and faster decisions, and manage people more easily. Still, it's a demanding, tough job that's not for everyone. If you like being on the inside track, however, and you're energetic and organized, you might be a good fit for the position of a TV assignment desk editor.

Many TV assignment editors started out as photographers, since being a TV photographer requires many of the same skills as being an assignment editor. You've got to be able to juggle multiple tasks, deal with breaking news, listen to scanners, and get news and camera crews out the door and to the scene of breaking news on time.

Pitfalls

Running an assignment desk is hard work, day after day. Each day is different in terms of news stories, but remains equally demanding and challenging. The work can be incredibly stressful, and the pay is lacking when compared to some other jobs in television. An assignment desk editor

Kim Deal, TV assignment desk editor

Kim Deal is a television assignment desk editor with station WYFF in Greenville, South Carolina. Before she moved into television, she worked as a radio news director. For Deal, every day is different, and even a routine day can turn crazy in a heartbeat, making for a considerable amount of pressure. Deadlines, especially, are a constant source of anxiety, she says. "There's plenty of pressure in meeting TV deadlines, because a TV deadline can be as soon as the very next minute," Deal says. "You may have to prepare to interrupt programming for breaking news, and you want to get on the air as soon as possible. That means getting your crews to the scene fast, getting your live trucks and your helicopter in place, and getting information—as quickly and accurately as possible."

Still, Deal very much enjoys her job. "You get to be at the center of all the action during breaking news, and during a routine day, you're planning out coverage for the next days to come," she says. "You make things happen and keep the newsroom running smoothly."

Deal suggests that if you're interested in becoming a TV assignment desk editor, you should pay close attention to detail and your surroundings, and learn as much as you can about a wide variety of topics. Also, she says, it's important to establish and maintain relationships with people who can provide information when you need it.

While the job is fast-paced and demanding, Deal says she has learned to keep her cool (usually, anyway). Panicking and coming unraveled, she says, just makes everyone else feel more pressured. Hysteria is contagious, she noted, especially when the pressure is really on. "You don't want to make yourself, or everyone around you, crazy," Deal says. "There's enough pressure without that."

often is an undervalued position within a newsroom.

Perks

A television assignment desk editor definitely knows what is going on. You have no choice but to be kept in the inner loop. Jobs in the news business are interesting, always changing, and there tends to be a great deal of energy in a newsroom. Newsroom staffs often become close and enjoy each other's company, making for a nice camaraderie.

Get a Jump on the Job

If your school has a TV studio and offers news or announcements before or during school, jump in and volunteer to help out. Learn to be organized and work at thinking one step ahead of whatever is going on at the time. You also could call your local television studio and ask if you could come in and observe how the newsroom works.

TV NEWS DIRECTOR

OVERVIEW

There's a fire in the local hospital, a bank robbery happening right down the block, and a two-car accident out on the highway. As the news director, it's your task to decide which reporters are going where to cover these late-breaking stories, where to send the cameras, and how to get it all pulled together for the next newscast.

You may think that the TV news is the bailiwick of the TV news anchor—but in fact, there's a lot more that goes on behind the scenes to bring you each day's newscast. In charge of it all is the station's news director, who functions sort of like the editor of a newspaper. This is a critically important job because news reports attract a large audience and account for a large proportion of the station's advertising revenue.

TV stations and networks broadcast a variety of programs, including national and local news, and stations produce their own news programs in their own studios. The news director is in charge of the TV news teams, including reporters, camera operators, and technicians, who typically travel in electronic news-gathering trucks to various locations to cover news stories.

When you get to the job each day, your responsibility is to supervise the newsroom while you coordinate that day's wire service reports, tape or film inserts, and stories from your individual newswriters and reporters in the field. As you're doing all this, you'll work with your assignment editor to assign stories

AT A GLANCE

Salary Range

The boss doesn't earn the most in broadcast journalism, often taking home less than TV anchors. Salaries vary widely depending on size of station and location, but may range from an average of $57,600 to $86,400; as a common rule, earnings of broadcast personnel are highest in large metropolitan areas. The top three markets may go as high as $250,000.

Education/Experience

A degree in broadcast journalism or similar major is required; some type of broadcasting experience is typically helpful. About 450 colleges offer formal programs in journalism and mass communications, including TV broadcasting, and some community colleges offer two-year programs in broadcasting. Broadcast trade schools offer courses that last six months to a year and teach TV announcing, writing, and production.

Personal Attributes

News directors need to be unflappable and able to handle enormous stress and meet daily deadlines.

Requirements

A degree in journalism or communications and experience in broadcast journalism.

Outlook

Employment in broadcasting is expected to grow by 9 percent through 2012. Factors contributing to the relatively slow rate of growth include industry consolidation, introduction of new technologies, and competition from other media outlets. Keen competition is expected for many jobs, especially in large metropolitan areas, due to the large number of job seekers attracted by the glamour of this industry. You'll have the best chance if you have a college degree in broadcasting, journalism, or a related field, as well as relevant work experience. You'll find many entry-level positions at smaller TV or radio stations; consequently, workers often must change employers, and sometimes relocate, to advance.

to news teams, sending the teams on location if necessary.

In this business, the buck stops with the news director, who's responsible for the news team of reporters, writers, editors, and newscasters, as well as the studio and mobile unit production crews. As the senior administrator in the newsroom, it's your responsibility to figure out what events to cover, and how and when they will be presented in a news broadcast.

Scott Atkinson, TV news director

Scott Atkinson first realized he was destined for the news biz when he realized he was buying the *Wall Street Journal* with his allowance because he wanted to read the feature stories on the front page. "Also, my dad sold hearses for a living," he recalls, "so we went to two national conventions for funeral directors. At one of them, I saw a guy who seemed to be having a really good time. Turns out he was from a trade magazine for the funeral industry called *Casket and Sunnyside.* It just seemed like it beat working!

"I felt like a lot of young people do—that I was different and didn't fit in. I was a pretty good writer from a young age, but I was shy and kind of awkward. Journalism gave me the kick in the pants I needed to get out into the world, meet people, learn to take chances."

On the way, Atkinson traveled from print to TV by way of radio—moves he says he made for personal reasons: He wanted to get back home. "Even though [newspapers, radio, and TV] have different requirements and require slightly different talents, it's all storytelling to me," he says. "Now with the Web, I get to dabble in all three!"

Today, Atkinson runs his station's news department, which means he's responsible for hiring employees, keeping track of the budget, and making sure everyone gets along. He's also responsible for the overall tone and look of the newscasts—is the station sensational or serious? Are the reporters investigators? How often are they "live"? Are they being fair? Atkinson also has to deal with more mundane questions, such as what color should the news set be, and does the anchorwoman's new suit look right on camera? Along with his staff, Atkinson also helps decide what stories get covered on a given day, and how they get covered. "My boss is the station's general manager, who is responsible for the entire station—and, obviously, for making sure we make money," Atkinson explains.

Atkinson is a journalism lifer—at 49 years old, he's been a journalist for 31 of those years. "For 24 years I was a reporter for newspapers and then for TV, and I loved telling stories," he says. "Now that I'm older, I don't regret a minute of the time I spent 'on the street,' but my biggest satisfaction these days comes from the young people I hire for their first jobs. I enjoy working with them, giving them a good start in journalism. My payoff is when they go onto bigger and better things."

As in any job, there's also a downside. "The least satisfying part of my job is that it's hard on my family life, sometimes, because the hours can be long," he says. But it's still a job he'd recommend. Young people should be able to write and take pictures or handle video. "Journalists coming up through the ranks in the next few years will have to be able to 'do it all' to get jobs," Atkinson predicts. "Besides, it's good for you—sometimes you see things with a camera that you missed when you were busy taking notes, and vice versa."

Broadcast employees may be eligible to join a union; the principal unions representing employees in broadcasting are the National Association of Broadcast Employees and Technicians (NABET), the International Alliance of Theatrical Stage Employees (IATSE), and the American Federation of Television and Radio Artists (AFTRA).

Pitfalls

This industry is noted for its high pressure and long hours, with constant pressure to maintain ratings. Working in live television is always a challenge and can be daunting and stressful. Long hours are almost a given for this job, including nights, weekends, and holidays. The news never takes a break, and as the TV news director, you don't, either.

Perks

For many people, the excitement of working in broadcasting compensates for the demanding nature of the jobs. If you really love journalism and news, and you enjoy being in the thick of the action, this could be a perfect job for you.

Get a Jump on the Job

If you're pursuing a career in broadcasting, you should probably get some initial experience working at college radio and TV stations or through internships at professional stations. Although these positions are usually unpaid, they sometimes provide college credit or tuition. More importantly, they provide hands-on experience and a competitive edge when applying for jobs. In this highly competitive industry, broadcasters are less willing to provide on-the-job training, and instead seek candidates who can perform the job immediately.

TV NEWS PRODUCER

OVERVIEW

If you like working without a net, producing a television news show might be just the job for you. You'll face the daily challenge of live television, where a hundred things can go wrong. And you'll be producing a show in which your best-laid plans will be turned topsy-turvy by breaking news. The good news is that there's never a dull moment. As a TV news producer, it'll be your job to make sure the newscast is full of interesting stories, flows smoothly, and keeps to a schedule. You're the one who gathers all the important pieces of a newscast and ties them together in an informative and eye-pleasing package. You'll work under an executive news producer, who hires personnel and sets the philosophy for how your station covers the news. Some stations want tabloid (sensational) news coverage. Others prefer straightforward news reporting. No matter the news philosophy, the producer's job will be pretty much the same.

You'll get to your station about five hours before your newscast. You'll start out by checking the wire services and other news sources to make sure you're up to date on local, national, and international news. Then you'll pick the top stories for your newscast and coordinate the work of reporters, photographers, and production assistants. As the day develops, you'll check for breaking news by monitoring police scanners and wire services and talking to your reporters. You'll write a lot of the stories that will be read by anchors and

AT A GLANCE

Salary Range
$20,000 to $70,000

Education/Experience
You should have a bachelor's degree in broadcast journalism or another communication field. Major news stations will want you to have at least two years' experience producing newscasts or news specials. You might learn production skills at a small station or start as an intern at a bigger station.

Personal Attributes
You must function well despite the pressure of producing live television news. You should enjoy working with others on your news team and be a strong communicator. And you'll need lots of energy and creativity.

Requirements
You must have excellent vision, with or without corrective lenses, and you can't be color-blind. You need excellent hearing and a clear voice. You need good writing and computer skills and should be able to type at least 45 words a minute.

Outlook
Television news keeps growing, thanks mainly to the increase in 24-hour news cable stations. There should always be jobs for those able to perform the difficult and varied tasks involved in producing a newscast.

reporters. Because you're often producing just a 30-minute newscast, you must carefully budget your time. You'll determine the sequence of stories and how much time should be spent on each. Because eye-catching graphics are important for a good newscast, you'll discuss ideas with your graphics department and show your anchors the graphics that will be used. You'll want to meet with your anchors and production staff before the newscast to assure a smooth, well-organized newscast. Many of the schedules will be routine. For the evening newscast, news, weather, and sports usually are given in that order. The early morning news goes immediately to traffic and weather reporters.

During a newscast, you'll be in the control room along with the news director. You'll have the last word on every-

Stephanie Cravens, TV news producer

It didn't take Stephanie Cravens long to realize that for a television news producer, technical difficulties may always be just seconds away. So whether she's producing a newscast or another show for KSHB, NBC's affiliate in Kansas City, she always goes on the air ready for anything. "I say a little prayer before every show," she says, smiling. "Please let my guest show up on time . . . please let me not lose my temper . . . please let my ratings be up every day." Those prayers aren't always answered, but Cravens has become accustomed to that, too.

Cravens was just one year removed from the University of Kansas in 1998 when she became a part-time news producer at KSHB. When the station beefed up its morning news in 2002, she produced a newscast from 4 to 7. She'd arrive at work at 11 p.m. and work all night. "The whole philosophy was: 'News while you slept,'" she says. "If you heard about something yesterday, there'd better be a good reason why you're hearing about it again. Chances are that while you slept, something happened that you need to know about. When we went to war in Iraq, because of the time difference, everything happened in the early hours. People getting up at 4 o'clock might be high-powered business people or people working a shift. The content changes as the audience changes. At 5 o'clock, parents start to get up, so you give them stuff that parents need to know. Traffic starts at 5:15. Morning newscasts are very similar. You go to your weather, your traffic person, then your news. The viewership is very fluid. You can't know what's going to be and that's part of the excitement."

During three years producing the morning news, Cravens got more excitement than she cares to remember. A power failure once left her studio entirely in the dark. Auto parts or TV equipment on news trucks broke down. Studio equipment died or ruined a tape. Film crews rushed to cover breaking news only to find out their truck was at a location that required satellite transmission but the NBC satellite wasn't available. "You never know what's going to happen," she says. "Everybody who's had this job has incidents. Like the time all the lights in the studio went out. You have a commercial break and decide what to do. You can't put black on the air for 20 minutes but the show must go on." By using a special camera that happened to be in the studio and moving the news anchors to a different location, Cravens and her staff were able to finish the newscast and make it presentable. Yet she wouldn't give up a live newscast even if she could. "I've done taped shows and going live gives you more adrenaline, makes more of a sense of urgency and makes you perform on your toes better than when you know you can do another take. You don't have a second chance. You have to be good under pressure, almost thrive on it, especially when you have breaking stories. You have to look ahead. My executive producer says, 'Prevent the train wreck before it happens.'"

Preparation and communication are the best means for a news producer to avoid the train. Segments need to stick to a tight schedule. "You constantly have to be conscious of time," Cravens says. "You have to be conscious of when the satellites are booked, when the window

thing aired in the newscast. You'll stay in constant communication with your anchors and reporters and remind them how long each story should take. You'll tell them when you're about to go in and out of commercial breaks, and you'll let everybody know when there's a sudden change in plans. Still, you can be sure that even after all your preparation, you'll be in store for some unpleasant surprises.

is open or closed. You may have to find something else to fill that spot and that sometimes puts a lot of pressure on the anchors or any other talent involved. There's a lot of communication involved on every program, from the assignment editors to the producers to the production staff and talent. If the producer is not in control and does not know what happens next, the anchor will be seen as the one not being prepared and you never want that to happen. Not only is the anchor listening to you, but also talking and reading something in front of them. As a producer, you have to be aware of that. It's much like a book. The producer doesn't write the entire book, but I put the chapters in order."

Cravens in 2005 was assigned to produce *Kansas City Live*, a new one-hour variety show about people and places in the metropolitan area. "It's for people looking to be entertained and informed on what the city is about," Cravens says. "It's about, 'What interesting things are going on in my community?' as opposed to, 'What's going on in my community and who got shot last night?'"

For *Kansas City Live*, Cravens can practically sleep in. She doesn't arrive at the studio until 6 a.m. "First, I make sure nothing horrible has happened [to the equipment] overnight," she says. "Then I double-check all the details. There's a lot of tease writing. I make a lot of callbacks. We have at least one meeting with the co-hosts and production staff." Cravens also books the show's guests several months in advance. So naturally, on the debut show, a guest didn't show up. He didn't realize he'd missed his appearance until friends asked him why they didn't see him on the show. Cravens had to adjust. "You let the other segments go longer," she explained. "You have to go in every day with a backup plan and it helps to know public relations people who you can ask, 'Who do you know who can be here in half an hour?'"

Cravens started at KSHB as an intern after working on the TV and radio stations at the University of Kansas. Her broadcasting education was invaluable, though much of what she learned is now obsolete. "Without that, I wouldn't have had the knowledge I needed for my internship," she says. "Looking back, almost everything's out of date. In college, we learned to splice tape. Now people don't have any idea what that is." To keep up to date, Cravens says, you can never stop learning. "You have to be open minded and listen to other people's ideas because you don't know everything," she says. "You're not the best out there and if you think you are, you're never going to improve."

Cravens has developed her career while she and her husband raised two daughters. Although *Kansas City Live* is a daily show, Cravens is on call some weekends and isn't able to take every holiday off. TV news work, clearly, involves more than stylish clothes and 30 minutes in the studio. "People need to understand we don't do this because we think it's glamorous," Cravens says. "We do it because it's what we like to do."

The football player who scored the winning touchdown may not be able to appear for the live interview you arranged. You might have to cancel that spot or delay it a few minutes and fill that spot with other news. You may encounter problems with the lighting, sound, tape, or transmission from your news trucks. As the producer, it will be up to you to make sure nobody panics and that the entire crew adjusts and keeps the newscast rolling as smoothly as possible. Your executive producer will evaluate the quality of your work and newscast, while the Nielsen ratings will estimate how many viewers are watching and how your show stacks up against the competition. If you don't like working in a pressure cooker, don't even think about producing the news.

Pitfalls

There are countless technical glitches that may make your job even more nerve-racking than usual. You'll often work nights, weekends, and holidays. The hours make it difficult to enjoy a normal family life.

Perks

You'll look forward to work every day because you'll love the challenge and satisfaction of producing a good live newscast. You'll enjoy the camaraderie of being part of a highly motivated team. You'll have a good outlet for your energy and creativity.

Get a Jump on the Job

Find a position on your university's TV station. Any news jobs will help you understand part of what's involved in producing the news. Watch all newscasts in your market. Note the different approaches and different people covering the news. Ask yourself which newscasts work best and why. How would you change them if you could?

TV NEWS REPORTER

OVERVIEW

You've probably seen them, standing in front of fire, flood, or political unrest, microphone in hand, calmly telling the story while on location or interviewing important figures or experts as part of the news.

A TV reporter's job is quite different from a news anchor (called, appropriately enough, "news reader" in Great Britain). While the anchor is usually expected simply to read the news or introduce taped segments, the TV reporter has to actually get out there and get the story, interview the usual suspects, and write the details for taping. The TV news reporter also gathers information from various sources, analyzes and prepares news stories, and reports on the air.

General-assignment reporters cover newsworthy events such as accidents, political rallies, visits of celebrities, or business stories as assigned. Large TV stations often assign reporters to gather news about specific topics, such as crime or education; other reporters specialize in an entire field, such as health, politics, foreign affairs, sports, theater, consumer affairs, social events, science, business, or religion. Investigative reporters cover stories that may take many days or weeks of information gathering. There's a lot of behind-the-scenes work that may not be apparent, but that takes up most of the reporter's time. Some stations use teams of reporters instead of assigning each reporter one specific topic, allowing reporters to cover a

AT A GLANCE

Salary Range

Salaries vary widely depending on the size and location of the station, and whether or not the position is unionized. TV news reporting is the entry level broadcast journalism job, with pay that is accordingly low—ranging from $19,000 to $22,000 at small-to-medium stations. When reporters move up to the 25 largest markets, their earnings become roughly comparable to those of daily newspaper reporters in such markets. The median for TV reporters in moderate-sized stations was about $54,000 to $150,000. Star newspaper reporters make a lot more, but they can be seen as more comparable to TV's anchors than its reporters.

Education/Experience

A degree in broadcast journalism or similar major is required; some type of broadcasting experience is helpful. About 450 colleges offer formal programs in journalism and mass communications, including TV broadcasting, and some community colleges offer two-year programs in broadcasting. Broadcast trade schools offer courses that last six months to a year and teach TV announcing, writing, and production.

Personal Attributes

Ability to work long, hard hours; meet deadlines; attention to detail; honesty and credibility. A nose for news, persistence, initiative, poise, resourcefulness, a good memory, and physical stamina are important, as is the emotional stability to deal with pressing deadlines, irregular hours, and dangerous assignments. TV reporters also need an excellent speaking voice without obvious regional accent, and a reasonably attractive appearance.

Requirements

Dedication to providing accurate and impartial news, because the job of serving the public is vital (and because untrue or libelous statements can lead to lawsuits). Broadcast reporters and news analysts must be comfortable on camera, and must be at

(continues)

AT A GLANCE *(continued)*

ease in unfamiliar places and with a variety of people.

Outlook

Employment in broadcasting is expected to increase almost 9 percent through 2012, or more slowly than the average for all industries, according to the U.S. Bureau of Labor Statistics. Factors contributing to the relatively slow rate of growth include industry consolidation, introduction of new technologies, and competition from other media outlets. Keen competition is expected for many jobs in large metropolitan areas because so many people are attracted by the glamour of this industry. You'll have the best chance if you have a college degree in broadcast journalism, communications, or a related field, as well as relevant work experience. Many entry-level positions are at smaller broadcast stations. To move up the ladder, you typically must get a job at a different TV station and relocate.

greater variety of stories. Such a news team may include reporters, editors, graphic artists, and photographers working together to complete a story.

News reporters are important to many TV stations because they attract a large audience and account for a large proportion of revenue. As a TV news reporter, a typical day would find you arriving at the station to find out what you might be covering that day. If there's an important meeting at the mayor's office, a big trial, or a hot school board meeting, you'll grab your notebook and take off on location with a camera crew. At the location, you may need to interview several different individuals, gathering important quotes and taping some of their comments. Certain

breaking news requires live on-air shots, which may include the reporter and subject in an interview. Many reporters enter information or write stories using laptop computers and electronically submit the material to their offices from remote locations. Otherwise, the story may be videotaped for later editing and airing at the next regular news show. Once you're back from location, you'll organize the material, determine the focus or emphasis, write the stories, and edit accompanying video material. At times, you may later tape an introduction to or commentary on their story in the studio.

TV reporters usually are assigned to a day or evening shift, but they sometimes have to change their work hours to meet a deadline or to follow late-breaking developments. Most reporters start at small broadcast stations as general assignment reporters or copy editors, covering court proceedings and civic and club meetings, and summarizing speeches. With experience, they report more difficult assignments or specialize in a particular field. Large stations rarely hire recent graduates; as a rule, they require new reporters to have several years of experience. Broadcast employees may be eligible to join a union; the principal unions representing employees in broadcasting are the National Association of Broadcast Employees and Technicians (NABET), the International Alliance of Theatrical Stage Employees (IATSE), and the American Federation of Television and Radio Artists (AFTRA).

Pitfalls

As any TV reporter will tell you, the main problems with this job are the hours and the pay. The news never stops, so you're

Meredith Jorgensen, TV reporter

For Meredith Jorgensen, life as a TV reporter for the midsize WGAL-TV in Lancaster, Pennsylvania, means that every single day is different. "You don't know what you'll be covering until you walk in the door," she says—but that's one of the best things about the job. "I meet new people every single day—three or four people I've never met before. I learn their names, what they do, and I get to learn a bit about them."

A Long Island native, she majored in broadcast journalism at Ithaca College in upstate New York, where she decided to combine her social personality and passion for current events into a career. After graduating, she first landed a job for Blue Ridge Cable in small-town Ephrata, Pennsylvania, anchoring the CNN Headline News Local Edition before moving up to the midsize TV station in central Pennsylvania.

At WGAL, Jorgensen has landed the graveyard shift, working from 3 p.m. to midnight. "So I get to cover anything that's going on anywhere at that time," she laughs. "Being a jack-of-all-trades has always been my theme," she says—and that's one thing she really likes about her job. "I get a little education on every story. I can go cover a story about doctors, lawyers, sewer systems, gardening, taxes—I'm not necessarily an expert on any of these, but I get to learn a little about each of them."

Basically, she loves to write and she considers herself a storyteller. "There are a lot of different ways to tell stories, but writing is the most important part of a storyteller's craft. I really like telling stories with pictures. It's a lot more compelling when you can see the burning building rather than just describing it in black and white ink in the newspaper."

In fact, it's the pictures that make the most compelling story, she believes—but it's her job to come up with the words to make those pictures understandable. It can be a frightening thing to stand in front of a camera on the scene and just tell people what the story is, without the benefit of teleprompters or notes. "It takes practice," she says. "It's very scary the first time you have to do that as a live shot. But after you do that a few times, the more you do it the more comfortable you become. It's empowering, and once you've mastered that, it's exciting when you can do it and do it well."

If you're thinking of being a TV reporter one day, Jorgensen recommends that you put a lot of emphasis on choosing the right college that can provide you with a good broadcast journalism program. "I went to a college that had a TV station so that I could practice my craft. It doesn't matter what your major is, if you're interested in a certain career you need to make sure to tailor your education to what you want to do."

It's also important to get as many internships as possible. "Internships are like keys, especially in broadcast journalism," she explains. "College broadcast organizations are different from working TV stations, so it's very, very important to have internships."

Jorgensen spent one of her internships at a Fox news channel in Manhattan, another at an NBC-TV station in London, England, and her last internship at the Long Island TV station in the town where she grew up. "Those were three very varied organizations that really gave me a good idea about what TV is all about," she says.

(continues)

often required to be on the job (especially when you first start out) on weekends, holidays, and evenings. When everyone else is home dishing up Thanksgiving dinner or opening the Christmas or Hanukkah gifts, you're out on the road with a notebook and a microphone. Competition can also be fierce. There's also a great deal of pressure to meet deadlines. Broadcasts sometimes are aired with little or no time for preparation. Finally, the job itself can sometimes be heartbreaking; there may be occasions when you need to interview grieving friends or family members about a tragedy and ask tough questions you'd rather avoid.

(continued)

It's also important to work on your writing; Jorgensen suggests budding TV journalists practice writing, and she highly recommends keeping a journal. "Take as many writing courses as you can," she says, "and grammar is absolutely imperative. You must know how to speak correctly and write correctly." This brings her to the topic of regional accents—a no-no in the world of TV journalism. "I grew up on Long Island, and other people told me I spoke funny," she laughs. "It's important to have a non-regional accent. Really, it's more to make it as least distracting for the viewer as possible. I've been practicing a long time to lose my Long Island accent."

It can certainly be exciting and even glamorous to be a local TV news reporter, but it's not all fun. "If you want to be a broadcast journalist, you have to have a passion for it, because there are a lot of really crummy parts about the job—the hours, the deadlines, the schedule, the pay. All my friends are teachers, and they don't work nights, weekends, and holidays—and I do. There are days when you're working on Christmas morning when your family is opening up presents." Although the more seniority you have the better, more reasonable your hours, "there are still days when people who have been there 25 years have to work. You know, we don't have a light switch at the station, because the lights never go off. And I eat lunch and dinner in the car, and I always get fast food. There's no lunch break," she laughs.

In addition to the long hours, salaries for TV reporters—at least in the beginning—aren't that high. "However, wages can go up exponentially depending on your talent and drive. There's a lot of paying dues [in the beginning]," she says.

Someday, Jorgensen dreams of being an anchor—the next step up on the career ladder for a TV journalist. "About 50 percent [of TV reporters] end up as anchors," she says, "and there's more prestige and more money as an anchor." Most TV reporters progress in their careers by moving on to a larger station, she explains.

"TV markets are numbered from one to 212, with 212 being the smallest market," she says. "What people try to do is to market climb. You aim for the top." WGAL is a 41, which is a very high market for a reporter under age 30, like Jorgensen. "We have four people under 25 here," she says. "It's a good, talented bunch."

All in all, the life of a TV reporter can be great. There's a lot of upward mobility, and it's certainly much easier for women to get into the field than it used to be. "It's easier for women and for minorities, because newsrooms want to be really diverse. Women are more than 50 percent of the population."

Perks

There's a lot of independence in this kind of work, and for people who love to write and to tell stories, it can be a thrilling occupation. Also, there's a certain amount of star "celebrity" status, even in small or local TV stations. You may be recognized on the street, which can be lots of fun. It can also be exciting to be among the first to witness major local and national events—not to mention meeting famous people.

Get a Jump on the Job

If you're pursuing a career in broadcasting, you should probably get some initial experience working at your high school or college radio and TV stations, or school paper. Alternatively, internships are another good learning tool. Although these positions are usually unpaid, they sometimes provide college credit or tuition. More importantly, they provide hands-on experience and a competitive edge when applying for jobs. In this highly competitive industry, broadcasters are less willing to provide on-the-job training, and instead seek candidates who can perform the job immediately.

TV NEWS VIDEOGRAPHER

OVERVIEW

TV news videographers, also known as news camera operators or electronic news gathering (ENG) operators, work with reporters and editors to capture news events that are later broadcast to viewers. The work—some of which must be done on very short notice and quite quickly—can be exciting, which makes it appealing to many.

That's not to say, however, that every day in the life of a TV news videographer is filled with excitement. If you think about the contents of your local television news, you'll probably recall a fair number of less-than-thrilling events, such as school board or municipal meetings, country fairs, and school sporting events. That's not to say that those events are not important or newsworthy, it's just that they're more predictable than breaking news such as a major traffic accident or a natural disaster.

TV news videographers at smaller and midsized stations usually are assigned to cover a variety of events. Videographers at large, metropolitan stations may have a more specialized area of coverage. Camera people for national news stations may be assigned to a particular beat, such as the White House, which means that most of your work would be confined to that location. TV networks also assign camera people to cover certain events, such as the Iraq war or the aftermath of Hurricane Katrina.

Camera operators for major TV networks may find themselves traveling exten-

AT A GLANCE

Salary Range

Earnings for a TV news videographer range from $22,640 to $56,400, according to government statistics.

Education/Experience

You'll probably need a college degree to land a job as a TV news videographer, although you may be able to accomplish that by completing a photography course at technical school. A telecommunications degree or another degree with components of both photography and journalism is preferable.

Personal Attributes

News camera operators must have good artistic ability and be energetic and agile. You must be able to think on your feet and respond quickly, as you'll need to get to the scene of breaking news and be ready to photograph events once you arrive. News people sometimes meet resistance from people they are trying to film or talk to, so you'll need to be aware of potential trouble. You should have good communication skills, be accurate, and detail oriented.

Requirements

Requirements will vary depending on where you work, but you'll probably need to have a valid driver's license and be able to operate a vehicle. You'll also need press credentials in order to access news scenes and other events.

Outlook

Jobs as TV news videographers are expected to increase between 10 and 20 percent through 2012. That job growth is considered average.

sively, sometimes into areas or situations that are unpleasant or even unsafe.

TV news videographers at any level must be able to work under pressure. It's not easy to hold a camera steady and stay

Chad Blimline, TV news videographer

One week out of every five, Chad Blimline finds it very difficult to make any plans outside of work. That's his on-call week, where he may be awakened at any time during the night to respond to a breaking news story.

Blimline works as a TV news videographer for the Allentown, Pennsylvania–based TV station WFMZ. Although he loves the work, the hours can be daunting.

His usual workday is from 8:30 a.m. until 6 p.m. Often, however, 6 stretches to 8 or 9, or even later. Then, there are the on-call weeks, when he never knows what will occur.

"Sometimes during those weeks I'll get called out for five out of seven nights," he says. "But, other weeks, I might not get called out at all. That's the thing, you never know if you're going to need to go, and if you do, how long it will take. It just makes it really hard to plan for anything."

Still, Blimline says he can't imagine doing any other job.

"It's just amazing to me that I get to have the variety of experiences that I do," Blimline says. "I've photographed from planes, covered major fires, grand opening events, and some great concerts and shows. I've also had to knock on the doors of parents whose child was murdered. You get a lot of highs and a lot of lows. But there's never two days that are alike."

Blimline graduated from the Pennsylvania State University with a degree in telecommunications. He calls himself a photojournalist, and his job, indeed, sometimes includes both interviewing and photographing news subjects.

If a news announcer needs a sound bite for a story, Blimline may be assigned to go out and get it. He's told the general framework of the story, and the particular part of it for which the announcer needs some feedback.

For instance, Blimline had recently returned to the office from an assignment at a new arts center. Members of the county's visitors bureau were touring the arts center, and Blimline was to get their reactions. Because there was not a reporter sent out with him, it was up to Blimline to ask people questions about the arts center and film their replies.

The same day, however, Blimline and a reporter from the station had visited a nature sanctuary at the other end of the county to get a story on people who visit the sanctuary at this time of year to witness the southern migration of hawks, falcons, and eagles. That type of assignment, he says, is very different from the first.

"When I'm with a reporter, I can pay a lot more attention to the photography and get much better shots," Blimline says. "And, it allows us to get much more in depth on a story. A photographer alone is good for collecting sound bites, but not for going in depth on a feature or a news story."

When asked which scenario he prefers, Blimline was noncommittal.

"They're both good," he says. "When I'm sent out on my own, I get to work independently, and I like that. But, there are more opportunities for really good work when I'm with a reporter, and that's really important to me."

He finds his work extremely satisfying, and enjoys seeing the fruits of his labors each day.

"Every day is different, and at the end of every day you get to watch what you've done that day. Some days, like those ones when you have to knock on a door, are incredibly hard, and you wonder what you're doing. But other days are so exhilarating and exciting and rewarding. I can't think of any job I'd rather be doing."

focused on your job when a major news event is unfolding in front of you. And, if you're on a tight deadline for getting your work edited and ready for broadcast, it might be necessary for you to edit raw footage at the scene so that you can relay it for broadcast.

Still, the appeal for many TV news videographers is that you never know what the day will bring, and you've got to be prepared to deal with whatever might occur. The standards for TV news coverage are high. Photographers and reporters provided real-time coverage of the events that unfolded on September 11, 2001, in New York City; Washington, D.C.; and Somerset, Pennsylvania. News crews were on the scene in Louisiana, Mississippi, and Alabama following Hurricane Katrina before the Federal Emergency Management Agency (FEMA) had a chance to respond.

Viewers have come to expect almost instant TV news coverage, and reporters and photographers have worked hard to satisfy that demand.

Nearly all TV news videographers started in small or midsized markets and worked their way up to larger ones. If you want to work for a large market, it's likely that you'll need to be willing to move.

New York is the largest television market in the country, followed by Los Angeles and then Chicago. If you want to make it big, you've got to be in a big market.

Pitfalls

TV news videographers often must work long hours, including nights and week-ends, and must be ready to work on short notice, when necessary. The work can be uncomfortable, and even dangerous, depending on circumstances. And TV videographers generally don't get rich from shooting news footage. You're likely to encounter some pretty unpleasant circumstances from time to time, and competition for jobs can be tough.

Perks

While some people might be put off by the thought of rushing out late at night to cover a major fire, a murder, or an approaching storm, TV camera operators seem to thrive on it. There's no question that the job can be exciting and exhilarating. People who work in newsrooms or out on beat are always up to date with what's going on, and two days are rarely alike.

Get a Jump on the Job

Video cameras aren't all that expensive and are a great way to start practicing taking live video. If your school has a TV studio, be sure to get involved and learn everything you can about operating the camera and the art of photography. Volunteer at your local television station, offering to help with whatever work needs to be done. Try to get a job in a camera or video store, join a photography club, and seek advice from anyone you meet who has some experience in this area.

TV WEATHER FORECASTER

OVERVIEW

Every day on national TV, the weather forecaster "stars" bring America the latest news about upcoming weather. Armed with charts, graphs, maps, and fancy Doppler radar, the forecaster plays a vital role in bringing information to viewers. It can be of enormous importance for many people to know what the day's weather will bring—such as the business traveler who needs to know whether a flight will likely be delayed, a family hoping to host an outdoor wedding, or to an entire community at risk for tornados, hurricanes, and other severe life-threatening weather events.

Since the advent of the primitive, short-range forecasts first used in the 1950s, the TV weather forecaster has come a long way. The current complex simulations can generate multi-level predictions extending more than a week into the future. Back in the 1960s, satellite imagery at best could only come up with static views of clouds, but today viewers enjoy animated details with 20/20 clarity. TV weather also features weather radars; back in the mid-1950s, radar was effective only at short ranges and with limited geographical coverage. Today, weather radar provides a continuous, real-time watch over virtually the entire continental United States. The new Doppler radars can provide not only advance warning of severe local storms but probe the atmosphere for everything from drizzle and snow flurries to wind shear. As computer technology has matured,

AT A GLANCE

Salary Range

It's difficult to predict the salary for a TV weather forecaster since it depends so much on the size of the station and the fame of the forecaster. A weather forecaster for a very small station in middle America makes far less than a national star such as Al Roker, weatherman for the *Today Show* on NBC. Excluding such well-known national weather "stars," incomes generally range from $30,200 to more than $60,200, depending on the size of the station.

Education/Experience

Some TV and radio weathercasters don't have a meteorology degree; instead, they study broadcast journalism and get their information from meteorologists to present on air. Many TV stations have both. Becoming a meteorologist requires a college degree in meteorology. Computer science courses, a strong background in mathematics and physics, and good communication skills are important to prospective employers. Some people get into meteorology by joining the armed forces instead of going to college, getting their training at various weather stations. Although you don't have to study broadcast journalism to be a TV weather forecaster, students who wish to become broadcast meteorologists for radio or television stations should develop excellent communication skills through courses in speech, journalism, and related fields.

Personal Attributes

Weather forecasters should be personable, comfortable on camera, and be able to handle lots of pressure both on- and off-air. While the day-to-day forecasting may seem ho-hum, sudden emergency weather situations, such as a sudden developing tornado or severe thunderstorm, requires the ability to get on camera fast to warn the TV audience and accurately predict the storm's path. This may require ignoring computer data if the weather forecaster's human understanding of weather differs.

(continues)

AT A GLANCE (continued)

Requirements

College degree in journalism, communications, or meteorology.

Outlook

Employment in broadcasting is expected to increase almost 9 percent through 2012, more slowly than the projected growth for all industries combined. Factors contributing to the relatively slow rate of growth include industry consolidation, introduction of new technologies, and competition from other media outlets. In particular, opportunities in weather forecasting in the broadcasting field are rare and highly competitive, making for very few job openings. Keen competition is expected for many jobs (especially in large metropolitan areas) because so many people are attracted by the glamour of this industry. You'll have the best chance if you have a college degree in meteorology with experience in broadcast journalism. Many entry-level positions are available at smaller broadcast stations. To move up the ladder, you typically must get a job at a different TV station and relocate.

weather prediction models became more and more sophisticated.

Every TV station in the country has some type of weather forecaster, ranging from part-time, fairly obscure jobs at small-market stations to celebrity positions at major networks and cable channels. When you first start out, you can expect to land a position at a small-market TV station, which can give you extensive opportunities to hone your craft and prepare to move up to a larger, major market position. These entry-level jobs usually offer a low salary and long or odd hours; weather takes no vacation, so forecasts need to be produced

on weekends and holidays, as well as during the normal workweek. Small station weather forecasters put up with this as a way of developing skills. Once you've established yourself as a broadcast meteorologist, many forecasters retain an agent who can help market their skills and help negotiate contracts.

If you're a trained meteorologist, you can generate forecasts and developing on-air graphics as just one component of larger news broadcasts. Forecasters at The Weather Channel, for example, analyze charts and computer models and assemble forecasts for all the cities in the United States and around the world, creating color-coded weather maps for broadcast. If you're not a trained meteorologist, you'll obtain your on-air material from private meteorological firms who support TV weather forecasting.

In addition, broadcast meteorologists may serve as environmental reporters, generating stories on a variety of earth topics. For example, an upcoming solar eclipse may prompt the weather caster to present a story about such phenomena and safe ways for viewers to observe the event. Other parts of the job may include forecast development for the Internet, or calling in weather reports to sister radio stations. In addition, broadcast meteorologists often are strongly linked to the community and are often asked to visit local classrooms to discuss the weather.

Weather reports are important to many television stations because they attract a large audience and account for a large proportion of revenue. Broadcast employees may be eligible to join a union; the principal unions representing employees in broadcasting are the National Association of Broadcast Employees and Technicians (NABET), the International Alliance of Theatrical Stage Employees (IATSE), and the American Federation of Television and Radio Artists (AFTRA).

Pitfalls

Because atmospheric science is a small field, relatively few colleges and universities offer degrees in meteorology or atmospheric science, although many departments of physics, earth science, geography, and geophysics offer atmospheric science and related courses. Prospective students should make certain that courses required by the National Weather Service and other employers are offered at the college they are considering. Starting out in weather forecasting means low salaries and long hours; it can take a long time to work your

Matt Ritter, TV weather forecaster

Ever since he can remember, TV meteorologist Matt Ritter has been interested in his surroundings. "Well, the weather is the ultimate surrounding," he says. "I noticed as a young boy it was always changing. But I didn't get interested in a scientific understanding of the weather until high school, when the Weather Channel first came on cable." Back in the 1980s when the Weather Channel debuted, the channel managed to work in a lot more scientific explanations about the weather, which is not always a good thing in TV, Ritter recalls. But that's what got him interested in the science behind the weather. "So I caught on to the explanations of why the weather was happening and I started learning. I simply ended up wanting to learn more," he says.

And so off he went to study meteorology at Millersville University in Millersville, Pennsylvania, where he worked with the Campus Weather Service and WIXQ-FM, the university radio station, as a disc jockey. Intent on landing a TV job, he began working while still a college senior as a behind-the-scenes assistant at WGAL-TV in Lancaster, Pennsylvania. Graduating with a B.S. in meteorology in 1992, he started working on-air at WGAL during the blizzard of 1993, providing viewers with updated information during the overnight hours. Later, he became the first meteorologist on the weekend editions of News 8 Today when the show premiered in 1995, moving on to the station's News 8 show at 6 p.m. and 11 p.m. on the weekends. Today, Ritter, who holds the Broadcasting Seal of Approval from the American Meteorological Society, provides the forecasts on News 8 at Noon Monday through Fridays. In addition, he maintains and develops the various weather computers the News 8 Storm Team uses. In this capacity, he typically works from about 10 a.m. until 7 p.m.—great hours, considering that most people in the TV weather business work from 2 a.m. until noon, or from 2 p.m. until midnight. "Shifts can change," he notes, "if you're working for someone else who's on vacation. If there is severe weather you may have to work all kinds of crazy, long hours."

The best thing about being a TV forecaster, Ritter says, is that "it's never the same thing two days in a row. Depending on what the weather is actually doing that day, each part of the job varies, and I really like the variety. I'm a combination of scientist, teacher, graphic artist, and comedian, kind of all at once."

way up. Promotion usually means you'll need to move to a larger station in a larger town.

Perks

If you really love meteorology or the weather, you enjoy helping others, and you're an outgoing type of person, this is the perfect job to combine all three aspects of your dream career. Being a TV forecaster can be exciting and every day is always different.

Get a Jump on the Job

If you find the weather fascinating and you're thinking about a career as a TV weather forecaster, join the American Meteorological Society as a student member—kids as young as elementary age can join as associate members. The AMS also offers internships and college scholarships, so it pays to learn a lot about this organization. Student members may buy weather-related discounted journals, books, and CD-ROMs, and subscribe to *Weatherwise* magazine at a 20 percent discount. Student members can also register for AMS conferences and workshops at a reduced rate, apply for fellowships and travel grants, and enjoy free access to online career information.

APPENDIX A: ASSOCIATIONS, ORGANIZATIONS, AND WEB SITES

ADVICE COLUMNIST

American Association of Sunday and Feature Editors
College of Journalism
1117 Journalism Building
University of Maryland
College Park, MD 20742-7111
(301) 314-2631
gseay@courant.org
http://www.aasfe.org

AASFE, founded in 1947, is an international organization of editors dedicated to the quality of features in newspapers. Gossip columnists are among the writers usually supervised by feature editors. The association supports its membership with an annual convention, a writing contest, regional workshops, and publications. The convention addresses such topics as how to use graphs, short copy blocks, and photo layouts with feature stories, and how to cover sex and pop culture without angering readers. AASFE sponsors contests that honor top feature stories and top feature sections, which present lifestyle, arts, and entertainment coverage with authority, energy, and wit. The association has established a Features Hall of Fame to honor the most outstanding feature writers.

AP WIRE SERVICE STAFFER

Associated Press Managing Editors
450 West 33rd Street
New York, NY 10001
(212) 621-1838
apme@ap.org
http://www.apme.com

APME is an association of editors at newspapers in the United States and Canada. It works closely with The Associated Press to foster journalism excellence and support a national network for the training and development of editors who will run multimedia newsrooms. APME has held a yearly conference since 1933 in various cities around the U.S. and Canada. APME is dedicated to the improvement, advancement, and promotion of journalism through members' own newspapers and through their relationship with the AP. APME is a key source of information and support for editors striving to produce vital, interesting newspapers day in and day out. Elected officers serve as national leaders speaking out on important issues in journalism.

AUTOMOTIVE WRITER

International Motor Press Association
4 Park Street
Harrington Park, NJ 07640
(201) 750-3533
info@impa.org
http://www.impa.org

The International Motor Press Association is an organization of professional automotive journalists and others representing the automotive industry. Its members meet for lunch once a month in New York City, where they listen to relevant speakers and network with one another and guests. The IMPA, which was founded nearly half a century ago, also sponsors a major event each year in connection with the New York International Automobile Show, and each fall holds Test Days, a two-day event during which members can test automobiles of nearly every kind.

CABLE TV SPORTS PERSONALITY

American Sportscasters Association
225 Broadway, Suite 2030
New York, NY 10007
(212) 227-8080
info@americansportscastersonline.com
http://americansportscastersonline.com

The ASA is dedicated to promoting, supporting, and enhancing the work of member sportscasters. It also provides information and guidance for those interested in becoming sportscasters. The association, founded in 1980, seeks to set high standards for ethics, integrity, and professional conduct. Through the ASA Hall of Fame and annual Hall of Fame Awards dinner, ASA recognizes achievements of outstanding sportscasters. It honors a Hall of Fame inductee, sportscasters of the year, and other standouts in the field as well as other individuals who've had an impact on society and the world of sports. The Hall of Fame was opened in 1998 and features rare memorabilia, the history of sports broadcasting since the 1920s, and an interactive display of sportscasting greats.

National Cable and Telecommunications Association
1724 Massachusetts Avenue, NW
Washington, DC 20036
http://www.ncta.com/

This association can provide descriptions of occupations in the cable industry and links to employment resources. The association (formerly the National Cable Television Association) is the principal trade association of the cable television industry in the United States. Founded in 1952, NCTA's primary mission is to provide its members with a strong national presence by providing a single, unified voice on issues affecting the cable and telecommunications industry. NCTA represents cable operators serving more than 90 percent of the nation's cable television households and more than 200 cable program networks, as well as equipment suppliers and providers of other services to the cable industry. In addition to offering traditional video services, NCTA's members also provide broadband services such as high-speed Internet access and telecommunications services such as local exchange telephone service to customers across the United States. NCTA hosts the industry's annual trade show, which serves as a national showcase for the cable industry's innovative services, including quality television programming, interactive television services, high-speed Internet access, and competitive local telephone service.

CARTOONIST

National Cartoonists Society
1133 West Morse Boulevard, Suite 201
Winter Park, FL 32789

(407) 647-8839
becca@crowseqal.com
http://www.reuben.org

The National Cartoonists Society was founded in 1946 after various cartoonists had become acquainted with one another while entertaining troops during World War II. The cartoonists discovered they very much enjoyed the company of one another, and decided to begin meeting on a regular basis. The group today includes more than 500 of the world's top, professional cartoonists. The purpose of the society is to advance the ideals and standards of professional cartooning, to create networking opportunities for members, and to provide information and assistance for aspiring cartoonists. Members regularly donate their talents to support worthwhile causes.

CROSSWORD PUZZLE CREATOR

Cruciverb.com
kmccann@cruciverb.com
http://www.cruciverb.com

The Cruciverb.com Web site is a resource center for crossword puzzle constructors. The site includes an e-mail list of members that's used to exchange information about crossword construction. Most discussions focus on American-style crossword puzzles rather than cryptics. The site includes puzzle databases and links to other crossword-related sites. Both professionals and beginners can collaborate on and benefit from cruciverb.com. Beginners can get tips on how to construct puzzles, devise themes, and use puns. They'll also learn why crossword editors change clues and how to use puns. Cruciverb.com is

supported by donations from constructors who use the site.

EDITORIAL WRITER

National Conference of Editorial Writers
3899 North Front Street
Harrisburg, PA 17110
(717) 703-3015
ncew@panews.org
http://www.ncew.org

Founded in 1947, the National Conference of Editorial Writers strives to promote high standards for editorial writers and improve the quality of editorial pages and broadcast editorials. Members benefit from educational opportunities such as low-cost workshops and seminars, critiquing services, foreign travel opportunities, an annual conference, an organizational magazine, and regional meetings. There also are e-mail discussion groups and an annual writing contest, with special categories for students.

FACT CHECKER (MAGAZINES)

American Society of Magazine Editors
Magazine Publishers of America
810 Seventh Avenue, 24th Floor
New York, NY 10019
(212) 872-3700
asme@magazine.org
http://www.magazine.org

The American Society of Magazine Editors (ASME) was founded in 1963, and has more than 850 members throughout the country. The organization serves as an advocate for magazine editors, particularly on issues relating to the First Amendment. It also provides forums for discussion among members. The society sponsors monthly roundtable lunches, annual national magazine awards, seminars and workshops, and a junior editorial seminar series.

Editorial Freelancers Association
71 West 23rd Street, Suite 1910
New York, NY 10010-4181
(212) 929-5400
http://www.the-efa.org/contactus.htm

EFA is a national organization, headquartered in New York City, whose members live and work all over the country and abroad. There are members in 45 of the United States, as well as Canada, England, France, India, Ireland, Israel, and Japan. EFA members are experienced in a wide range of professional skills, subject areas, and media. Nearly half are from outside the New York tristate region, but because they don't usually attend NYC-area events, they enjoy lower membership dues.

FOREIGN CORRESPONDENT

National Press Club
529 14th Street, NW, 13th Floor
Washington, DC 20045
http://npc.press.org

The Club provides people who gather and disseminate news a center for the advancement of their professional standards and skills, the promotion of free expression, mutual support, and social fellowship. The National Press Club has been a part of Washington life for more than 90 years. Its members have included 17 consecutive Presidents of the United States—from Theodore Roosevelt to Bill Clinton.

Society of Professional Journalists
Eugene S. Pulliam National Journalism Center
3909 North Meridian Street
Indianapolis, IN 46208
(317) 927-8000
spj@link2000.net
http://www.spj.org

SPJ is dedicated to the perpetuation of a free press. The society aims to promote the flow of information; maintain constant vigilance to protect First Amendment guarantees of freedom of speech and of the press; stimulate high standards and ethical behavior in journalism; foster excellence among journalists; encourage diversity in journalism; be the preeminent membership organization of journalists, and encourage a climate in which journalism can be practiced freely. SPJ holds an annual convention that features group discussions and hands-on training. It publishes Quill, a magazine for professional journalists. SPJ awards two annual summer internships for students who wish to research and write about freedom of information issues.

GOSSIP COLUMNIST

American Association of Sunday and Feature Editors
College of Journalism
1117 Journalism Building
University of Maryland
College Park, MD 20742-7111
(301) 314-2631
gseay@courant.org
http://www.aasfe.org

AASFE, founded in 1947, is an international organization of editors dedicated to the quality of features in newspapers. Gossip columnists are *among the writers usually supervised by feature editors. The association supports its membership with an annual convention, a writing contest, regional workshops, and publications. The convention addresses such topics as how to use graphs, short copy blocks and photo layouts with feature stories, and how to cover sex and pop culture without angering readers. AASFE sponsors contests that honor top feature stories and top feature sections, which present lifestyle, arts, and entertainment coverage with authority, energy, and wit. The association has established a Features Hall of Fame to honor the most outstanding feature writers.*

HELICOPTER NEWS REPORTER

Professional Helicopter Pilots Association
PO Box 7059
Burbank, CA 91510
(213) 891-3636
info@phpa.org
http://www.phpa.org

The PHPA aims to help helicopter pilots promote safety, education, and communications among each other, as well as to improve their methods of operation. It seeks to provide a forum for members and promote community relations between the public and pilots and the rest of the helicopter industry. The PHPA was established more than 25 years ago to provide a forum for pilots to share experiences and create a safer flying environment. The association has since branched out to become a pilot networking forum and the main contact group for many government agencies and private groups that seek out information and opinions on helicopter operations.

PHPA cosponsors an annual Helicopter Awareness Day, an air show held at several airports to share access and information about helicopters with the public. It schedules general membership meetings, which feature guest speakers, throughout the year. An annual safety seminar held each April emphasizes media relations and public safety. PHPA publishes a newsletter, Main Rotor.

HOROSCOPE COLUMNIST

United Feature Syndicate Newspaper Enterprise Association
200 Madison Avenue
New York, NY 10016
(212) 293-8500
http://www.unitedfeatures.com

Organization that develops and markets 150 comic strips and editorial features worldwide, including Peanuts, Dilbert, Pearls Before Swine, Get Fuzzy, Miss Manners, *and* Nat Hentoff, *through the United Feature Syndicate and Newspaper Enterprise Association.*

HUMOR COLUMNIST

American Humor Studies Association
3800 Lindell Boulevard
St. Louis, MO 63108-3414
mcintire@slu.edu
http://www.americanhumor.org

AHSA is dedicated to the study of American humor. The association is an affiliate of the Modern Language Association and American Literature Association and presents convention programs at the annual conventions of both societies and also sponsors programs elsewhere. Any member of the MLA or ALA may attend AHSA meetings and submit papers for consideration at annual MLA or ALA meetings. *To present a paper during an AHSA session, the presenter must be a current member. Membership benefits include the semiannual newsletter,* To Wit, *and the annual journal,* Studies in American Humor. *The association also sponsors the Charlie Awards, given for lifetime achievement in service to AHSA and for outstanding research in American humor.*

Dave Barry.com: FAQ for Students
http://www.davebarry.com/faq_for_students.html

Web site of Miami Herald *humor columnist Dave Barry. This helpful Web page gives Dave's answers to a variety of questions from students.*

INVESTIGATIVE REPORTER

Investigative Reporters and Editors, Inc.
138 Neff Annex
Missouri School of Journalism
Columbia, MO 65211
(573) 882-2042
info@ire.org
http://www.ire.org

IRE provides educational services to reporters, editors, and others interested in investigative journalism and works to maintain high professional standards. IRE compiles data, tip sheets, past stories, and other information to help cover such stories as hurricanes, earthquakes, wars, space exploration, and power blackouts. IRE's resource center includes more than 20,000 print and broadcast stories and more than 2,000 tip sheets. As a promoter of journalism education, IRE

offers training opportunities throughout the year, ranging from national conferences and regional workshops to weeklong boot camps and on-site newsroom training. Costs are on a sliding scale and fellowships are available to many of the events.

MAGAZINE EDITOR

American Society of Magazine Editors
Magazine Publishers of America
810 Seventh Avenue, 24th Floor
New York, NY 10019
(212) 872-3700
asme@magazine.org
http://www.magazine.org

The American Society of Magazine Editors (ASME) was founded in 1963, and has more than 850 members throughout the country. The organization serves as an advocate for magazine editors, particularly on issues relating to the First Amendment. It also provides forums for discussion among members. The society sponsors monthly roundtable lunches, annual national magazine awards, seminars and workshops, and a junior editorial seminar series.

MOVIE CRITIC

Internet Movie Critics Association
http://www.geocities.com/Hollywood/Studio/5713

The Internet Movie Critics Association is an online organization that posts movie reviews and related materials from members, who are comprised of professional and nonprofessional movie critics. Critics are carefully screened before they are admitted as members. You can read movie reviews and articles on the Web site.

NATIONAL GEOGRAPHIC PHOTOGRAPHER

National Press Photographers Association
3200 Croasdaile Drive, Suite 306
Durham, NC 27705
(919) 383-7246
http://www.nppa.org/

Founded in 1946, the NPPA is open to professional news photographers and all others whose occupation has a direct professional relationship with photojournalism. NPPA hosts five national workshops of various types on everything from general photography and motivation to television photography and technology. NPPA has a job information bank that posts several job openings every week, along with an e-commerce store, and an AV library. It publishes materials that are in demand by researchers, students, instructors, and photojournalists all over the world.

North American Nature Photography Association
10200 West 44th Avenue, Suite 304
Wheat Ridge, CO 80033-2840
(303) 422-8527
http://www.nanpa.org

NANPA is a nonprofit organization of a wide range of individuals and corporations from all over North America and the world with an interest in nature photography. NANPA's mission is to promote the art and science of nature photography as a way to communicate nature appreciation and environmental protection, to educate and inspire, gather and disseminate information, and develop standards for all persons interested in the field of nature photography. NANPA is an organization for nature "photography," not just nature "photographers." NANPA's membership is open to anyone interested in photography of nature and the environment, specifically professional and serious nature photographers, editors and publishers, educators, students, corporations, and others.

NEWSPAPER BUREAU CHIEF

National Press Club
529 14th Street, NW, 13th Floor
Washington, DC 20045
http://npc.press.org

The Club provides people who gather and disseminate news a center for the advancement of their professional standards and skills, the promotion of free expression, mutual support, and social fellowship. The National Press Club has been a part of Washington life for more than 90 years. Its members have included 17 consecutive Presidents of the United States—from Theodore Roosevelt to Bill Clinton.

OMBUDSMAN

Organization of News Ombudsmen
PO Box 120191
San Diego, CA 92112
(619) 293-1525
ono@uniontrib.com
http://www.newsombudsmen.org

Formed in 1980, ONO maintains contact with news ombudsmen worldwide and organizes conferences to discuss news practices and a wide range of issues connected with ombudsman work. ONO strives to help journalism achieve high ethical standards in news reporting; establish and refine standards for the job of news ombudsman; help expand the position of ombudsman in newspapers and elsewhere in the media; provide a forum for exchanging experiences, information, and ideas among members; develop contacts with publishers, editors, and other professional organizations; provide speakers for special interest groups, and respond to media inquiries. Yearly ONO meetings include seminars, panels, and speakers on topics of special interest to ombudsmen.

POLITICAL COLUMNIST

National Society of Newspaper Columnists
1345 Fillmore Street, Suite 507
San Francisco, CA 94115
(415) 563-5403
director@columnists.com
http://www.columnists.com

The National Society of Newspaper Columnists was started in 1977 when a columnist from the Norfolk Virginian-Pilot sent out letters inviting other columnists to get together informally to talk about their work. A small group of columnists showed up, and the society was born. It has grown in both size and diversity since then, now including columnists of every sort. The society works to promote high ethical standards among columnists, holds an annual

meeting, and provides educational opportunities and advice for members.

RADIO DISC JOCKEY

American Disc Jockey Association
20118 North 67th Avenue
Suite 300-605
Glendale, AZ 85308
(888) 723-5776
office@adja.org
http://www.adja.org

The American Disc Jockey Association has chapters in 22 states. It offers a variety of services to members, including special rates on property insurance, reduced price rental car offers, a newsletter, and legal and accounting services. The intent of the organization is to provide support, education, and networking opportunities for disc jockeys in all parts of the United States.

RADIO REPORTER

National Association of Broadcasters
1771 N Street, NW
Washington, DC 20036
(202) 429-5300
nab@nab.org
http://www.nab.org

NAB is a full-service trade association that represents the interests of free, over-the-air radio and television broadcasters. For radio members, NAB offers a broad range of educational events and awards programs. The association sponsors The Radio Show, an annual event that features conference sessions and networking opportunities. NAB also sponsors an annual broadcast *management conference and an executive development program. NAB sponsors the Marconi Awards, which recognize stations and on-the-air personalities for excellence in radio; the Crystal Radio Awards, which recognize stations for outstanding community service; and the National Radio Award, which recognizes an outstanding leader in the radio industry. NAB also sponsors a Broadcasting Hall of Fame.*

The Association of Independents in Radio
328 Flatbush Avenue, #322
Brooklyn, NY 11238
(888) 937-2477
http://www.airmedia.org

AIR is a diverse membership alliance of independent producers, programmers, marketers, stations, networks, media arts centers, attorneys, teachers, and anyone committed to creativity and vision in public radio. AIR members live and work in the United States, Canada, and many other parts of the world.

SPORTS COLUMNIST

National Society of Newspaper Columnists
1345 Fillmore Street, Suite 507
San Francisco, CA 94115
(415) 563-5403
director@columnists.com
http://www.columnists.com

The National Society of Newspaper Columnists was started in 1977 when a columnist from the Norfolk Virginian-Pilot sent out letters inviting other columnists to get together informally to talk about their work. A small group of columnists showed up, and the society

was born. It has grown in both size and diversity since then, now including columnists of every sort. The society works to promote high ethical standards among columnists, holds an annual meeting, and provides educational opportunities and advice for members.

TV NEWS ANCHOR

National Association of Broadcasters Career Center
1771 N Street, NW
Washington, DC 20036
http://www.nab.org

NAB is a full-service trade association that promotes and protects the interests of radio and television broadcasters in Washington and around the world. NAB is the broadcaster's voice before Congress, federal agencies, and the courts. They also serve a growing number of associate and international broadcaster members. NAB's legislative success is the direct result of political involvement by local broadcasters, who help educate policymakers about the realities of radio and television. This association can also provide information on broadcasting education and scholarship resources.

TV NEWS ASSIGNMENT DESK EDITOR

Radio-Television News Directors Association
1600 K Street, NW, Suite 700
Washington, DC 20006-2838
(202) 659-6510
rtnda@rtnda.org
http://www.rtnda.org

The Radio-Television News Directors Association (RTNDA) is a worldwide organization, representing electronic news personnel in 30 countries. It has more than 3,000 members, including news directors, editors, news associates, students, and educators. The organization was founded in 1946 with the purpose of establishing standards for reporting and gathering news. It works to protect First Amendment rights and provides benefits for members. There are student chapters of the RTNDA.

TV NEWS DIRECTOR

Radio-Television News Directors Association
1600 K Street, NW, Suite 700
Washington, DC 20006-2838
(202) 659-6510
rtnda@rtnda.org
http://www.rtnda.org

RTNDA is the world's only professional organization exclusively serving the electronic news profession. It's made up of more than 3,000 news directors, news associates, educators, and students. It was founded in 1946 as a grassroots organization to set standards for news gathering and reporting. The association seeks to uphold those standards, even as news techniques and technologies have changed dramatically. RTNDA and its foundation honor professional achievements in electronic journalism through awards, scholarships, fellowships, and internship programs. The association holds an annual convention, in conjunction with the National Association of Broadcasters. This features exhibitions of news-gathering technologies and discussions of newsroom issues.

TV NEWS PRODUCER

Radio-Television News Directors Association
1600 K Street, NW, Suite 700
Washington, DC 20006-2838
(202) 659-6510
rtnda@rtnda.org
http://www.rtnda.org

RTNDA is the world's only professional organization exclusively serving the electronic news profession. It's made up of more than 3,000 news directors, news producers, news associates, educators, and students. It was founded in 1946 as a grassroots organization to set standards for news gathering and reporting. The association seeks to uphold those standards, even as news techniques and technologies have changed dramatically. RTNDA and its foundation honor professional achievements in electronic journalism through awards, scholarships, fellowships, and internship programs. The association holds an annual convention, in conjunction with the National Association of Broadcasters. This features exhibitions of news-gathering technologies and discussions of newsroom issues.

TV NEWS REPORTER

Council on Education in Journalism and Mass Communications
University of Kansas
School of Journalism
Stauffer-Flint Hall

Lawrence, KS 66045-7575
http://www.ku.edu/~acejmc

The Accrediting Council on Education in Journalism and Mass Communications, or ACEJMC, is the agency responsible for the evaluation of professional journalism and mass communications programs in colleges and universities. This council can provide a list of schools with accredited programs in broadcast journalism.

National Association of Broadcast Employees and Technicians
Communications Workers of America
501 Third Street, NW
Washington, DC 20001
http://www.nabetcwa.org

A union devoted to helping workers employed in the broadcasting, distributing, telecasting, recording, cable, video, sound recording, and related industries in North America. You can find careers information and links to employment resources on the Web site.

TV NEWS VIDEOGRAPHER

National Press Photographers Association
3200 Croasdaile Drive, Suite 306
Durham, NC 27705
(919) 383-7246
info@nppa.org
http://www.nppa.org

With a membership of more than 10,000, the National Press Photographers Association (NPPA) includes working photographers, student representatives, and life members. It represents both still and television photographers. The organization works to protect freedom

of the press, and to instill high standards of professionalism among working photographers. Members benefit from educational opportunities, contact with other members, opportunities for trips, and opportunities for discounts on equipment and insurance.

TV WEATHER FORECASTER

American Meteorological Society
45 Beacon Street
Boston, MA 02108-3693
(617) 227-2425
http://www.ametsoc.org

The American Meteorological Society promotes the development and dissemination of information and education on the atmospheric and related oceanic and hydrologic sciences and the advancement of their professional applications. Founded in 1919, AMS has a membership of more than 11 000 professionals, professors, students, and weather enthusiasts. AMS publishes nine atmospheric and related oceanic and hydrologic journals—in print and online—sponsors more than 12 conferences annually, and offers numerous programs and services.

International Association of Broadcast Meteorology
http://www.iabm.org

An organization designed to enhance the status of broadcast meteorology around the world, and to communicate the views of weather broadcasters about the supply of weather information.

National Weather Association
1697 Capri Way

Charlottesville, VA 22911-3534
(434) 296-9966
http://www.nwas.org

The National Weather Association is a professional nonprofit association, incorporated in Washington, DC, in 1975 mainly to serve individuals interested in operational meteorology and related activities. It has grown to over 2,800 members, 50 corporate members, and over 250 subscribers, including many colleges, universities, and weather service agencies. International members and subscribers number over 50.

APPENDIX B: ONLINE CAREER RESOURCES

This volume offers a look inside a wide range of unusual and unique careers that might appeal to someone interested in jobs in the media. While it highlights general information, it's really only a quick snapshot of this very large field. The entries are intended to merely whet your appetite, and provide you with some career options you may never have known existed.

Before jumping into any career, you'll want to do more research to make sure that it's really something you want to pursue. You'll most likely want to learn as much as you can about the careers in which you are interested. That way, as you continue to research and talk to people in those particular fields, you can ask informed and intelligent questions that will help you make your decisions. You might want to research the education options for learning the skills you'll need to be successful, along with scholarships, work-study programs, and other opportunities to help you finance that education. And, you might want answers to questions that weren't addressed in the information provided here. If you search long enough, you can find just about anything using the Internet, including additional information about the jobs featured in this book.

✳ **A word about Internet safety:** The Internet is a wonderful resource for networking. Many job and career sites have forums where students can interact with other people interested in and working

in that field. Some sites even offer online chats where people can communicate with each other in real time. They provide students and jobseekers opportunities to make connections and to begin to lay the groundwork for future employment. But as you use these forums and chats, remember that anyone could be on the other side of that computer screen, telling you exactly what you want to hear. It's easy to get wrapped up in the excitement of the moment when you're on a forum or in a chat, interacting with people who share your career interests and aspirations. But be cautious about what kind of personal information you make available on the forums and in the chats; never give out your full name, address, or phone number. And never agree to meet with someone you've met online.

SEARCH ENGINES

When looking for information, there are lots of search engines that will help you to find out more about these jobs, along with others that might interest you. While you might already have a favorite search engine, you might want to take some time to check out some of the others that are out there. Some have features that might help you find information not located with the others. Several engines will offer suggestions for ways to narrow your results, or related phrases you might want to search along with your search results. This is handy if you are having trouble locating exactly what you want.

Another good thing to do is to learn how to use the advanced search features of your favorite search engines. Knowing that might help you to zero-in on exactly the information for which you are searching without wasting time looking through pages of irrelevant hits.

As you use the Internet to search information on the perfect career, keep in mind, that like anything you find on the Internet, you need to consider the source from which the information comes.

Some of the most popular Internet search engines are:

AllSearchEngines.com
www.allsearchengines.com
This search engine index has links to the major search engines along with search engines grouped by topic. The site includes a page with more than 75 career and job search engines at http://www.allsearchengines.com/careerjobs.html.

AlltheWeb
http://www.alltheweb.com

AltaVista
http://www.altavista.com

Ask.com
http://www.ask.com

Dogpile
http://www.dogpile.com

Excite
http://www.excite.com

Google
http://www.google.com

HotBot
http://www.hotbot.com

LookSmart
http://www.looksmart.com

Lycos
http://www.lycos.com

Mamma.com
http://www.mamma.com

MSN Network
http://www.msn.com

My Way
http://www.goto.com

Teoma
http://www.directhit.com

Vivisimo
http://www.vivisimo.com

Yahoo!
http://www.yahoo.com

HELPFUL WEB SITES
The Internet is a wealth of information on careers—everything from the mundane to the outrageous. There are thousands of sites devoted to helping you find the perfect job for your interests, skills, and talents. The sites listed here are some of the most helpful ones that the authors came across and/or used while researching the jobs in this volume. The sites are listed in alphabetical order. They are offered for your information, and are not endorsed by the authors.

All Experts
http://www.allexperts.com

"The oldest & largest free Q&A service on the Internet," AllExperts.com has thousands of volunteer experts to answer your questions. You can also read replies to questions asked by other people. Each expert has an online profile to help you pick someone who might be best suited to answer your question. Very easy to use, it's a great resource for finding experts who can help to answer your questions.

America's Career InfoNet
http://www.acinet.org

A wealth of information! You can get a feel for the general job market; check out wages and trends in a particular state for different jobs; and learn more about the knowledge, skills, abilities, and tasks for specific careers; and learn about required certifications and how to get them. You can search more than 5,000 scholarship and other financial opportunities to help you further your education. A huge career resources library has links to nearly 6,500 online resources. And for fun, you can take a break and watch one of nearly 450 videos featuring real people at work; everything from custom tailors to engravers, glassblowers to silversmiths.

Backdoor Jobs
http://www.backdoorjobs.com

This is the Web site of the popular book by the same name, now in its third edition. While not as extensive as the book, the site still offers a wealth of information for people looking for short-term opportunities: internships, seasonal jobs, volunteer vacations, and work abroad situations. Job opportunities are classified into several categories: Adventure Jobs, Camps, Ranches & Resort Jobs, Ski Resort Jobs, Jobs in the Great Outdoors, Nature Lover Jobs, Sustainable Living and Farming Work, Artistic & Learning Adventures, Heart Work, and Opportunities Abroad.

Boston Works—Job Explainer
http://bostonworks.boston.com/globe/ job_explainer/archive.html

For nearly 18 months, the Boston Globe *ran a weekly series profiling a wide range of careers. Some of the jobs were more traditional. Others were very unique and unusual. The profiles discuss an "average" day, challenges of the job, required training, salary, and more. Each profile gives an up close, personal look at that particular career. In addition, the Boston Works Web site (http://bostonworks.boston.com) has a lot of good, general employment-related information.*

Career Planning at About.com
http://careerplanning.about.com

Like most of the other About.com topics, the career planning area is a wealth of information, and links to other information on the Web. Among the excellent essentials are career planning A-to-Z, a career planning glossary, information on career choices, and a free career planning class. There are many great articles and other excellent resources.

Career Prospects in Virginia
http://www3.ccps.virginia.edu/career_ prospects/default-search.html

Career Prospects is a database of entries with information on more than 400 careers. Developed by the Virginia Career Resource Network, the online career information resource of the Virginia Department of Education, Office of

Career and Technical Education Services, it was intended as a source of information about jobs "important to Virginia," but it's a great source of information for anyone. While some of the information such as wages, outlook, and some of the requirements may apply only to Virginia, the other information for each job, such as like what's it like, getting ahead, skills, and the links will be of help to anyone interested in that career.

Career Voyages
http://www.careervoyages.gov

"The ultimate road trip to career success," sponsored by the U.S. Department of Labor and the U.S. Department of Education. This site features sections for students, parents, career changers, and career advisors with information and resources aimed to that specific group. The FAQ offers great information about getting started, the high-growth industries, how to find your perfect job, how to make sure you're qualified for the job you want, tips for paying for the training and education you need, and more. Also interesting are the hot careers and the emerging fields.

Dream Jobs
http://www.salary.com/careers/layouthtmls/crel_display_Cat10.html

The staff at Salary.com takes a look at some wild, wacky, outrageous, and totally cool ways to earn a living. The jobs they highlight include pro skateboarder, computer game guru, nose, diplomat, and much more. The profiles don't offer links or resources for more information, but they are informative and fun to read.

ESPN Careers
http://www.joinourteam.espn.com/joinourteam

Our mission here at ESPN is to attract and retain the most talented people by fostering an environment for them to thrive in their work efforts. Use the search criteria to view a list of ESPN job openings and to apply online. To ensure you view all opportunities please select the "select all" in the location field. If you don't find a current opening, you can set up a job search agent or submit a resume to be considered when an opportunity becomes available. Thank you for your interest in the Worldwide Leader in Sports.

Find It! in DOL
http://www.dol.gov/dol/findit.htm

A handy source for finding information at the extensive U.S. Department of Labor Web site. You can "Find It!" by broad topic category, or by audience, which includes a section for students.

Fine Living: *Radical Sabbatical*
http://www.fineliving.com/fine/episode_archive/0,1663,FINE_1413_14,00.html#Series873

The show Radical Sabbatical on the Fine Living network looks at people willing to take a chance and follow their dreams and passions. The show focuses on individuals between the ages of 20 and 65 who have made the decision to leave successful, lucrative careers to start over, usually in an unconventional career. You can read all about these people and their journeys on the show's Web site.

Free Salary Survey Reports and Cost of Living Reports
http://www.salaryexpert.com

Based on information from a number of sources, Salary Expert will tell you what kind of salary you can expect to make for a certain job in a certain geographic location. *Salary Expert has information on hundreds of jobs; everything from your more traditional white- and blue-collar jobs, to some unique and out of the ordinary professions like acupressurist, blacksmith, denture waxer, taxidermist, and many others. With sections covering schools, crime, community comparison, community explorer, and more, the moving center is a useful area for people who need to relocate for training or employment.*

Fun Jobs

http://www.funjobs.com

Fun Jobs has job listings for adventure, outdoor, and fun jobs at ranches, camps, ski resorts, and more. The job postings have a lot of information about the position, requirements, benefits, and responsibilities so that you know what you are getting into ahead of time. And, you can apply online for most of the positions. The Fun Companies link will let you look up companies in an A-to-Z listing, or you can search for companies in a specific area or by keyword. The company listings offer you more detailed information about the location, types of jobs available, employment qualifications, and more.

Girls Can Do

http://www.girlscando.com

"Helping girls discover their life's passions," Girls Can Do has opportunities, resources, and a lot of other cool stuff for girls ages 8 to 18. Girls can explore sections on Outdoor Adventure, Sports, My Body, The Arts, Sci-Tech, Change the World, and Learn, Earn, and Intern. In addition to reading about women in all sorts of careers, girls can explore a wide range of opportunities and information that will help them grow into strong, intelligent, capable women.

Great Web Sites for Kids

http://www.ala.org/gwstemplate.cfm?section=greatwebsites&template=/cfapps/gws/default.cfm

Great Web Sites for Kids is a collection of more than 700 sites organized into a variety of categories, including animals, sciences, the arts, reference, social sciences, and more. All of the sites included here have been approved by a committee made up of professional librarians and educators. You can even submit your favorite great site for possible inclusion.

Hot Jobs: Career Tools

http://www.hotjobs.com/htdocs/tools/index-us.html

While the jobs listed at Hot Jobs are more on the traditional side, the Career Tools area has a lot of great resources for anyone looking for a job. You'll find information about how to write a resume and a cover letter, how to put together a career portfolio, interviewing tips, links to career assessments, and much more.

Job Descriptions & Job Details

http://www.job-descriptions.org

Search for descriptions and details for more than 13,000 jobs at this site. You can search for jobs by category or by industry. You'd probably be hard pressed to find a job that isn't listed here, and you'll probably find lots of jobs you never imagined existed. The descriptions and details are short, but it's interesting and fun, and might lead you to the career of your dreams.

Job Hunter's Bible

http://www.jobhuntersbible.com

This site is the official online supplement to the book What Color Is Your Parachute? A Practical Manual for Job-Hunters and Career-Changers, *and is a great source of information with lots of informative, helpful articles and links to many more resources.*

Job Profiles
http://www.jobprofiles.org

A collection of profiles in which experienced workers share about rewards stressful parts of the job; basic skills the job demands; challenges of the future; and advice on entering the field. The careers include everything from baseball ticket manager to pastry chef and much, much more. The hundreds of profiles are arranged by broad category. While most of the profiles are easy to read, you can check out the How to browse JobProfile. org section (http://www.jobprofiles.org/ jphowto.htm) if you have any problems.

Major Job Web sites at Careers.org
http://www.careers.org/topic/01_jobs_ 10.html

This page at the careers.org Web site has links for more than 40 of the Web's major job-related Web sites. While you're there, check out the numerous links to additional information.

Monster Jobs
http://www.monster.com

Monster.com is one of the largest, and probably best known, job resource sites on the Web. It's really one-stop shopping for almost anything job-related that you can imagine. You can find a new job, network, update your resume, improve your skills, plan a job change or relocation, and so much more. Of special interest are the Monster: Cool Careers

(http://change.monster.com/archives/ coolcareers) and the Monster: Job Profiles (http://jobprofiles.monster.com) where you can read about some really neat careers. The short profiles also include links to additional information. The Monster: Career Advice section (http://content.monster.com/) has resume and interviewing advice, message boards where you can network, relocation tools and advice, and more.

Occupational Outlook Handbook
http://www.bls.gov/oco

Published by the U.S. Department of Labor—Bureau of Labor Statistics, the Occupational Outlook Handbook *(sometimes referred to as the OOH) is the premiere source of career information. The book is updated every two years, so you can be assured that the information you are using to help make your decisions is current. The online version is very easy to use; you can search for a specific occupation, browse through a group of related occupations, or look through an alphabetical listing of all the jobs included in the volume. Each of the entries will highlight the general nature of the job, working conditions, training and other qualifications, job outlook, average earning, related occupations, and sources of additional information. Each entry covers several pages and is a terrific source to get some great information about a huge variety of jobs.*

Online Sports.com Career Center—Jobs in Sports
http://www.onlinesports.com/pages/ CareerCenter.html

The Online Sports career center is a resource of sports-related career opportunities and a resume bank for potential employers within the many segments of the sports and recreation industries.

Online Sports.com Sports Career Planning

http://www.onlinesports.com/sportstrust

The Online Sports career planning center is a resource of sports-related career opportunities and a resume bank for potential employers within the many segments of the sports and recreation industries.

The Riley Guide: Employment Opportunities and Job Resources on the Internet

http://www.rileyguide.com

The Riley Guide is an amazing collection of job and career resources. Unless you are looking for something specific, one of the best ways to maneuver around the site is with the A-to-Z Index. You can find everything from links to careers in enology to information about researching companies and employers. The Riley Guide is a great place to find just about anything you might be looking for, and probably lots of things you aren't looking for. But, be forewarned, it's easy to get lost in the A-to-Z Index, reading about all sorts of interesting things.

JobsInSports.Com

http://www.jobsinsports.com/subscribe. cfm

This Internet-based employment service is dedicated to helping you find a sports job, packed with job databases listing hundreds of jobs in the areas of sports marketing, sports media, sales, health & fitness, computers and high-tech, and administration/management. There's

also an internship center specifically listing sports internships available for job seekers looking to gain experience, a sports contacts area with names and contact information for all of the major sports franchises, and a resume posting area where you can list your own resume.

USA TODAY Career Focus

http://www.usatoday.com/careers/dream/ dreamarc.htm

Several years ago, USA TODAY ran a series featuring people working in their dream jobs. In the profiles, people discuss how they got their dream job, what they enjoy the most about it, they talk about an average day, their education backgrounds, sacrifices they had to make for their jobs, and more. They also share words of advice for anyone hoping to follow in their footsteps. Most of the articles also feature links where you can find more information. The USATODAY.Com Job Center(http://www.usatoday.com/money/ jobcenter/front.htm) also has links to lots of resources and additional information.

Women Sports Jobs

http://www.womensportsjobs.com/ default.htm

This Web site is designed to help women find jobs in sports—sales, marketing, broadcasting, PR, coaching, officiating, health/fitness, athletic administration, event management, journalism, sporting goods, and more! The database is divided into 12 different industry categories, including Professional Teams, College Athletics, Sporting Goods Broadcast & Media, Sports Events, Recreation, Professional Services, Sports Associations, Sports Venues, Sports

Technology/Internet, and High School Sports.

CAREER TESTS AND INVENTORIES

If you have no idea what career is right for you, there are many resources available online that will help assess your interests and maybe steer you in the right direction. While some of the assessments charge a fee, there are many out there that are free. You can locate more tests and inventories by searching for "career tests," "career inventories," or "personality inventories," Some of the most popular assessments available online are:

Campbell Interest and Skill Survey (CISS)
http://www.usnews.com/usnews/edu/careers/ccciss.htm

Career Explorer
http://careerexplorer.net/aptitude.asp

Career Focus 2000 Interest Inventory
http://www.iccweb.com/careerfocus

The Career Interests Game
http://career.missouri.edu/students/explore/thecareerinterestsgame.php

The Career Key
http://www.careerkey.org

CAREERLINK Inventory
http://www.mpc.edu/cl/cl.htm

Career Maze
http://www.careermaze.com/home.asp?licensee=CareerMaze

Career Tests at CareerPlanner.com
http://www.careerplanner.com

FOCUS
http://www.focuscareer.com

Keirsey Temperament Test
http://www.keirsey.com

Motivational Appraisal of Personal Potential (MAPP)
http://www.assessment.com

Myers-Briggs Personality Type
http://www.personalitypathways.com/type_inventory.html

Princeton Review Career Quiz
http://www.princetonreview.com/cte/quiz/default.asp

Skills Profiler
http://www.acinet.org/acinet/skills_home.asp

READ MORE ABOUT IT

The following sources and books may help you learn more about media careers.

GENERAL CAREERS

U.S. Bureau of Labor Statistics, *Occupational Outlook Handbook, 2006–07*. Available online at http://www.bls.gov/oco/

Culbreath, Alice N., and Saundra K. Neal. *Testing the Waters: A Teen's Guide to Career Exploration*. New York: JRC Consulting, 1999.

Edwards, Christina. *Gardner's Guide to Finding New Media Jobs Online*. Herndon, Va.: Garth Gardner Company, 2003.

Farr, Michael, LaVerne L. Ludden, and Laurence Shatkin. *200 Best Jobs for College Graduates*. Indianapolis, Ind.: Jist Publishing, 2003.

Fogg, Neeta, and Paul Harrington, Thomas Harrington. *College Majors Handbook with Real Career Paths and Payoffs: The Actual Jobs, Earnings, and Trends for Graduates of 60 College Majors*. Indianapolis, Ind.: Jist Publishing, 2004.

Kent, Simon. *Careers and Jobs in the Media*. New York: Gardners Books, 2005.

Krannich, Ronald L., and Caryl Rae Krannich. *The Best Jobs for the 1990s and into the 21st Century*. Manassas Park, Va.: Impact Publications, 1995.

Levinson, Harry. *Designing And Managing Your Career (Advice from the Harvard Business Review)*. Cambridge, Mass.: Harvard Business School, 2000.

Mannion, James. *The Everything Alternative Careers Book: Leave the Office Behind and Embark on a New Adventure (Everything: School and Careers)*. Boston: Adams, 2004.

McKinney, Anne. *Real-Resumes for Media, Newspaper, Broadcasting and Public Affairs Jobs*. Fayetteville, N.C.: Prep Publishing, 2002.

Seguin, James. *Media Career Guide: Preparing for Jobs in the 21st Century*. New York: St. Martins, 2005.

ADVICE COLUMNIST

Stern, Paige. *For God's Sake, Don't Watch Porn For Pointers: And 101 Other Scraps Of Advice From America's Crankiest Advice Columnist*, The Nuisance Lady. New York: Harper, 1997.

AP WIRE SERVICE STAFFER

Mooney, Brian, and Barry Simpson. *Breaking News: How the Wheels Came off at Reuters*. Oxford, U.K.: Capstone Ltd., 2003.

Schwartz, Jerry. *Associated Press Reporting Handbook*. New York: McGraw-Hill, 2001.

AUTOMOTIVE WRITER

Dinkel, John. *Road & Track Illustrated Automotive Directory*. Cambridge, Mass.: Bentley Publishers, 2000.

Julty, Sam. *How Your Car Works*. New York: HarperCollins, 1974.

CABLE TV SPORTS PERSONALITY

Freeman, Michael. *ESPN: The Uncensored History*. New York: Taylor Trade Publishing, 2002.

Olbermann, Keith, and Dan Patrick. *The Big Show*. New York: Pocket Books, 1998.

CARTOONIST

Glasbergen, Randy. *How to be a Successful Cartoonist*. Cincinnati: North Light Books, 1996.

Hall, Robin. *Cartoonists' and Illustrators' Trade Secrets*. Boston: A&C Black, 2002.

Marchant, Steve. *The Cartoonist's Workshop*. London: Collins & Brown, 2004.

CROSSWORD PUZZLE CREATOR

Newman, Stan. *A Plethora of Crosswords: 500 Challenging Puzzles*. New York: Gramercy Books, 2005.

Pulliam, Tom, and Clare Grundman. *New York Times Crossword Puzzle Dictionary*. New York: Random House Puzzle & Games, 1999.

EDITORIAL WRITER

Casey, Maura, and Michael Zuzel. *Beyond Argument: A Handbook for Editorial Writers*. Harrisburg, Pa.: National Council of Editorial Writers, 2001.

Sloan, William David, and Laird B. Anderson. *Pulitzer Prize Editorials: America's Best Editorial Writing 1917-1993*. Ames, Iowa: Iowa State University Press, 1994.

FACT CHECKER (MAGAZINES)

Marek, Richard, with Leslie T. Sharpe and Irene Gunther. *Editing Fact and Fiction: A Concise Guide to Book Editing*. New York: Cambridge University Press, 1994.

Morrish, John. *How to Develop and Manage a Successful Publication*. Oxford, U.K.: Routledge, 2003.

Stainton, Elsie Myers. *The Fine Art of Copyediting*. New York: Columbia University Press, 2002.

White, Jan V. *Editing by Design: For Designers, Art Directors, and Editors—The Classic Guide to Winning Readers*. New York: Allworth Press, 2003.

FOREIGN CORRESPONDENT

Geyer, Georgie Anne. *Buying the Night Flight: The Autobiography of a Woman Foreign Correspondent*. Chicago: University of Chicago Press, 2001.

Goodman, Alan, and John Pollack. *The World on a String: How to Become a Freelance Foreign Correspondent*. New York: Owl Books, 1997.

GOSSIP COLUMNIST

Gabler, Neal. *Winchell: Gossip, Power and the Culture of Celebrity*. New York: Vintage Books, 1995.

Hopper, Hedda. *The Whole Truth and Nothing But*. New York: Doubleday, 1963.

HELICOPTER NEWS REPORTER

Padfield, Randall R. *Learning to Fly Helicopters*. New York: McGraw-Hill Professional, 1999.

Vasquez, Tim. *Storm Chasing Handbook*. Garland, Tex.: Weather Graphics Technologies, 2002.

HOROSCOPE COLUMNIST

George, Llewellyn, with Stephanie Jean Clement and Marylee Bytheriver. *Llewellyn's New A To Z Horoscope Maker & Interpreter*. St. Paul, Minn.: Llewellyn Publications, 2003.

Arroyo, Stephen, and Jerilynn Marshall. *Chart Interpretation Handbook: Guidelines for Understanding the Essentials of the Birth Chart*. Sebastopol, Calif.: CRCS Publications, 1990.

HUMOR COLUMNIST

Barry, Dave. *Dave Barry's Greatest Hits*. New York: Ballantine Books, 1997.

Fiel, Jared. *Fumbling Thru Fatherhood*. Greeley, Colo.: ATJA Books, 2004.

INVESTIGATIVE REPORTER

Woodward, Bob, and Carl Bernstein. *All The President's Men*. New York: Simon & Schuster, 1994.

Weiner, Tim. *Blank Check: The Pentagon's Black Budget*. New York: Warner Books, 1990.

MAGAZINE EDITOR

Morrish, John. *How to Develop and Manage a Successful Publication*. Oxford: Routledge, 2003.

White, Jan V. *Editing by Design: For Designers, Art Directors, and Editors—The Classic Guide to Winning Readers*. New York: Allworth Press, 2003.

MOVIE CRITIC

Haberski, Raymond J., Jr. *It's Only a Movie! Films and Critics in American Culture*. Lexington, Ky.: University Press of Kentucky, 2001.

Null, Christopher. *Five Stars! How to Become a Film Critic, the World's Greatest Job*. San Francisco: Sutro Press, 2005.

NATIONAL GEOGRAPHIC PHOTOGRAPHER

Burian, Peter, and Bob Caputo. *National Geographic Photography Field Guide: Secrets to Making Great Pictures*. Washington, D.C.: National Geographic, 1999.

National Geographic Society. *National Geographic Photography Field Guide: People and Portraits*. Washington, D.C.: National Geographic Society, 2002.

NEWSPAPER BUREAU CHIEF

Harrower, Tim. *Newspaper Designer's Handbook with CD-ROM*. New York: McGraw-Hill, 2001.

Kovach, Bill, and Tom Rosenstiel. *The Elements of Journalism: What Newspeople Should Know and The Public Should Expect*. New York: Three Rivers Press, 2001.

Schwartz, Jerry. *Associated Press Reporting Handbook*. New York: McGraw-Hill, 2001.

OMBUDSMAN

Fallows, James. *Breaking the News: How the Media Undermine American Democracy.* New York: Vintage Books, 1997.

Mnookin, Seth. *Hard News: The Scandals at the New York Times and Their Meaning for American Media.* New York: Random House, 2004.

POLITICAL COLUMNIST

Digregorio, Charlotte. *You Can Be a Columnist: Writing and Selling Your Way to Prestige.* Portland, OR: Civetta Press, 1993.

McCabe-Cardoza, Monica. *You Can Write a Column.* Cincinnati, Ohio: Writer's Digest Books, 2000.

RADIO DISC JOCKEY

Fresh, Chuck. *How To Be A DJ: Your Guide to Becoming a Radio, Nightclub, or Private Party Disc Jockey.* Melbourne, Fla.: Brevard Marketing, 1999.

Slaney, Charles. *The DJ Handbook.* Norfolk, U.K.: PC Publishing, 2002.

RADIO REPORTER

Crouse, Chuck. *Reporting for Radio.* Los Angeles: Bonus Books, 1992.

Gordon, George N. *On-the-spot Reporting; Radio Records History.* New York: J Messner, 1967.

SPORTS COLUMNIST

Albom, Mitch. *Live Albom: The Best of Detroit Free Press Sports Columnist Mitch Albom.* Detroit: Detroit Free Press, 1988.

Eskenazi, Gerald. *A Sportswriter's Life: From the Desk of a New York Times Reporter.* St. Louis, Mo.: University of Missouri Press, 2004.

Zigel, Vic. *Sunday Punch: Raspberries Strawberries Steinbrenners & Tysons Famed Sports Columnist Takes His.* East Rutherford, N.J.: Plume, 1991.

TV NEWS ANCHOR

Bachman, John F. *Beyond the Facts: Faith Sees the Deepest Truth—Reflections of a TV News Anchor.* Minneapolis: Kirk House Publishers, 2005.

McCoy, Michelle. *Sound and Look Professional On Television and the Internet: How to Improve Your On-Camera Presence.* Los Angeles: Bonus Books, 2000.

TV NEWS ASSIGNMENT DESK EDITOR

Pearlmann, Donn. *Breaking into Broadcasting: Getting a Good Job in Radio or TV—Out Front or Behind the Scenes.* Los Angeles: Bonus Books, 1986.

Trost, Scott, and Gail Resnik. *All You Need to Know About the Movie and TV Business; Fifth Edition.* New York: Fireside Press, 1996.

TV NEWS DIRECTOR

Kalbfeld, Brad. *Associated Press Broadcast News Handbook.* New York: McGraw Hill, 2000.

Kovach, Bill. *The Elements of Journalism: What Newspeople Should Know and The Public Should Expect.* New York: Three Rivers Press, 2001.

TV NEWS PRODUCER
Shook, Frederick. *Television Field Production and Reporting.* Boston: Allyn & Bacon, 2004.

Smith, Dow. *Power Producer: A Practical Guide to TV News Producing.* Washington, D.C.: Radio-Television News Directors Association, 2004.

TV NEWS REPORTER
Block, Mervin. *Writing Broadcast News—Shorter, Sharper, Stronger.* Los Angeles: Bonus Books, 1997.

Freedman, Wayne. *It Takes More Than Good Looks To Succeed at TV News Reporting.* Los Angeles: Bonus Books, 2003.

TV NEWS VIDEOGRAPHER
Lindekugel, D.M. *Shooters: TV News Photographers and Their Work.* Westport, Conn.: Praeger Publishers, 1994.

Ray, Charles. *The Life of a Network Newsreel Cameraman.* Casa Del Ray: Self-published, 2001.

TV WEATHER FORECASTER
Ahrens, C. Donald. *Meteorology Today: An Introduction to Weather, Climate, and the Environment.* Florence, Ky.: Brooks-Cole, 2002.

Stull, Roland B. *Meteorology for Scientists and Engineers: A Technical Companion Book to C. Donald Ahrens' Meteorology Today.* Florence, Ky.: Brooks-Cole, 2002.

Ackerman, Steven, and John A. Knox. *Meteorology: Understanding the Atmosphere.* Florence, Ky.: Brooks-Cole, 2004.

INDEX

Page numbers in **bold** indicate major treatment of a topic.

A